Protecting children from depression

Seven strategies for the primary prevention of depression

A HANDBOOK FOR PARENTS, TEACHERS AND COUNSELLORS

by

Andrew Willoughby

D0263777

FOURTH EDITION
2007

Published by Community Wellbeing Press
First Edition 2004
Second Edition 2004
Third Edition 2005
Fourth Edition 2007

UNITED KINGDOM
29A The Avenue, St Margaret's, London TW1 1QU
Email: Andrewwilloughby7@googlemail.com

AUSTRALIA
2-8 Ennis Road, Milson's Point, Sydney 2061
Telephone: 1 300 131 392
Email: dcrompton@gotraining.com.au

ISBN 0-9547691-0-4

Printed and bound in China

Contents

This book is dedicated to
Kate and Jason
and to
Kevin and Jean

List of illustrations and diagrams

Appendix

Acknowledgements

Many people have helped me to write this book. By far the most important are those children and young adults who killed themselves. I came to know their friends and relatives, and my sad and angry tears are nothing compared to their dry-eyed grief which will not go away. The recurring question: "What could I have done to prevent it?" – that question drives this book; to find and spell out what a parent, teacher, counselor or community can do to protect their children from getting depressed or suicidal.

At the outset I want to acknowledge that I am not a doctor or psychologist; I am an educator and community development worker, with a particular interest in how communities and organisations nurture wellbeing and transmit wellbeing skills to individuals and families, and how families nurture wellbeing. For several years I taught communication and relationship skills with the Family Life Movement, but my intense interest in protecting children and adults from depression developed while coordinating an Australian youth suicide prevention project, Project X.

I am especially indebted to the children, youth and townsfolk of Kyogle who created and participated in Project X. The community had experienced a tragic surge in youth suicides and several people decided to design a new kind of programme to develop and trial strategies for the primary prevention of depression and suicide in children and young people. Rather than wait until individual children were depressed, and then try and identify and treat them, which is often too difficult because people mask their distress, we worked on strategies to strengthen the community's ability to consciously nurture the wellbeing and sense of morale of all children and youth.

This project was funded by the Australian federal government in 1997 and 1998. It was very successful, reducing the youth suicide rate to zero in the local government area, and won the New South Wales Premier's Award in 1998.

These strategies which we developed can be applied in schools, individual families and in whole communities.

In particular, I want to acknowledge and thank Linda Woodrow, whose research into youth suicide formed the theoretical basis of Project X; Heidi Green and Michael Brown, whose vision, social entrepreneurship and sheer intelligence established the project. I want to acknowledge the students and staff of Kyogle High School for their vital participation, generosity and idealism. I want to also acknowledge the Kyogle Council, particularly the Mayor, Val Johnston, and Council staff for being so determined to make the town and the shire more nurturing and inclusive for youth. A special acknowledgement must go to David and Valerie Lake, who published *TKN, The Kyogle News*, which ran numerous stories and photos showing the many creative contributions which local schoolchildren were thinking up and making to the community, often in new partnerships with established organisations. I was inspired and encouraged by the many community organizations, religious congregations and local businesses who participated so generously. They demonstrated that it is possible for ordinary people in an ordinary community to change the culture of the community to protect and enhance the well-being of children and youth.

I would like to honour several writers and scientific thinkers whose works gave me inspiration, knowledge and powerful conceptual tools. First, and foremost, is Emile Durkheim, one of the founders of sociology, whose sociological study of suicide, *Le Suicide*, published over 100 years ago laid the enduring foundations for understanding and preventing depression and suicide. He showed that different social groups produce stable individual rates of suicide and that these vary according to the degree of social integration and moral regulation. The most recent statistical analyses of rates of suicide and depression confirm his findings. All the discoveries in neurobiology will enable us to penetrate the social biochemistry of depression. Depression is a social fact because the human brain and its biochemistry evolved to be socially organized. Durkheim's gift is yet to be fully unwrapped. John Maynard Keynes, with his insight that full employment is not the automatic natural consequence of the operation of the market, led me, by analogy, to the realization that mental health and well-being are not automatic products of social groups, with depression being an individual 'illness'. E.O. Wilson gave me the crucial bridge between sociology and biology with *Sociobiology* (1975) and challenged me to find biological foundations for joy, love and wisdom, with his book *Consilience*. The neuroscientist Antonio Damasio provided me with my first understanding of how the brain is structured and organized. Edward de Bono taught me about creating concepts, and Robert Fritz in his book *The Path of Least Resistance* showed me the structural nature of creative action, which forms the dynamic core of primary prevention – continually co-creating well-being.

Three other wonderful books helped me a great deal: Robert Putnam's masterpiece *Bowling Alone* showed the essential link between social integration and individual well-being and the importance of helping each generation create their own social capital in their own home-towns, their own communities. *The Tipping Point*, Malcolm Gladwell's brilliant book, showed me the way humans continually watch the social context and adapt to its signals. In *A Passion For Excellence*, Tom Peters gave me the invaluable concept of the lead user, the idea that in any group, people's varying levels of willingness to try new ideas can be seen as a bell curve, and, to initiate change in any group, you find the people at the thin leading edge of the bell curve, and work with them. They are the lead users, and others in the group then follow their lead.

I want to thank Wendy Sanford who has done an excellent job creating diagrams and layout. I am indebted to Kerry James for so generously creating the detailed drawings and models of the brain and the limbic system. I am most grateful to my daughter, Cassie Willoughby, for hours of word processing and work on the graphics, and to Jeanette Rai for her support and encouragement, and hundreds of conversations exploring and clarifying strategies and ideas.

For all the improvements to this edition, I wish to thank my editor, Rodney Peel, whose gentle clarity has both calmed and invigorated me, and my bearded designer, Peter Moore, who has created the new look. I want to thank Lynne Earnshaw for her many hours preparing the computer document – and stabilizing my hyperactive pdf files without recourse to Ritalin.

There are two people without whom I would not have written this book. The first is my life coach, Christina Grant, and the second is my spiritual teacher, Gangaji. I offer them both my grateful thanks.

For medical and scientific input I want to thank Dr. Graham Mussared, Dr. Jonine Penrose-Wall and child psychologist Allan Andreasen, while for practical and moral support I want to thank my dear friend, Chris Burgess, and all the men of Lismore Men's Group.

Introduction

The primary aim of this book is to show you how you can prevent children from developing depression, and, secondly, how to help them recover from it.

There are two forms of depression:

1 **Natural short-term depression** Natural depression is any low mood – which may last from a few minutes to a maximum of two weeks. The key feature is that the person recovers their normal energy and good humour naturally.

2 **Clinical long-term depression** Clinical or long-term depression is any depression which lasts longer than two weeks. The key feature is that the person finds it very difficult or impossible to recover by themselves. It is this form of depression which is increasing in children and in adults around the world.

What this book offers

This book gives you a detailed understanding of depression, a clear model of well-being, and a tested set of practical strategies which will help you to nurture well-being and prevent depression taking hold.

Second, you can use the information in this book to clarify the well-being deficits which may make particular children vulnerable to depression.

Third, you can use the strategies in this book to help rebuild well-being in those children who are depressed – and prevent depression recurring.

Fourth, you can use the model and the framework of strategies to strengthen well-being in a family, a whole school, or a community.

Parents, teachers, schools and health professionals now, more than never, need to share understanding and strategies to protect children from depression and directly create well-being. This book will help you turn children away from depression. It contains seven strategies which you can use straight away to eliminate causes of depression and make children happier and more socially and emotionally secure.

It is much better to prevent children from developing depression, than to wait until they are depressed and then treat the depression. Rates of childhood depression have never been higher – and they are rising more rapidly than adult depression, according to figures published by professor Robert Lane, of Yale University in his 2000 book, *The Loss of Happiness in Market Democracies*.

We can no longer assume that well-being happens naturally. In some areas researchers have reported rates of childhood depression of 25%. Welfare systems in many cases do not have the funding or staff to meet the needs of those large numbers, and families and schools are bearing the brunt of this epidemic. One of the great challenges that we face is to shift from a Welfare State to a Well-being State, so that we are able to consciously nurture well-being and build these skills into communities, families and children.

Defining depression

1   Natural short-term depression

Depression is not primarily a medical term; it simply means being in low spirits, feeling flat, unhappy and hopeless, or defeated. For a time, we lose our power and we lose our joy. It is natural to feel depressed when we are rejected, when we lose someone we love,   when some expectation or dream of ours fails, or when we feel that we are oppressed and have no freedom or control.

A central feature of natural short-term depression is that we have resilience – the ability to endure the suffering and then regain our happiness, vitality and optimism. This resilience is partly learnt and partly given to us by those who notice and care about us. Families, communities, schools and organisations vary enormously in their abilities to teach and provide this critical capacity of resilience.

Of itself, depression is not bad – quite the reverse in fact. It is valuable because it makes us stop and think, contemplate what has happened and reassess what we really value. We become more realistic in our perceptions and assessments. It gives us a chance to learn valuable lessons and make new choices. And it brings out the love and sympathy of those who care for us and builds enduring bonds. We only develop compassion because we all experience suffering at different times, and resonate with the pain we see in another person's face or hear in their tone of voice. As a social animal, we do not feel okay until those people we really care about feel happy again.

2   Clinical long-term depression

Clinical depression is a name often given to ongoing low mood, unhappiness and loss of interest in life. It is also called major depression. We are not designed to be able to stay depressed for very long, without losing our resilience. We quickly lose our ability to bounce back.

Clinical depression sets in after about two weeks of continuous hopelessness and low spirits. Yet adults often lead such pressurised and complex lives that it is easy for them to not really notice much about how a child is feeling over two weeks. At the same time, children may feel so accepting of the pressure and complexity- so used to it- that they don't pay much attention to their own feelings, or are too busy meeting expectations and deadlines to do anything about their depression. In these situations, depression can build up quietly over time. Our culture, which is competitive, rational and materialistic, puts very little value on the vital, delicate work of sharing grief or being intimately helpful. This builds stress as unacknowledged losses accumulate, and natural, short-term depressions solidify and intensify into clinical long-term depression.

The term clinical depression wrongly suggests that depression is a biological illness like measles or tuberculosis. It is not. It is a myth that depression is primarily a biological illness or genetically based.

Clinical depression is not an illness caused by a chemical imbalance in the brain. Rather, the depression causes changes to brain chemistry. When the social and psychological causes of the depression are persistent and unchanged, then this altered brain chemistry becomes stable and the depression becomes long-term. The good news is that 80% of people with clinical depression get completely better without any treatment within six months. However 20% are still clinically depressed two years later.

Children are very vulnerable to these natural feelings of depression, because they have so little power and so few resources, and yet are so emotionally alive. They form emotional attachments much more quickly and easily than adults, and yet have far less power to control and nurture these desires, affections and friendships. Girls, with their generally higher emotional intelligence than boys and lower status and freedoms in most cultures, suffer feelings of depression more often and more deeply than boys. Boys and young males have higher suicide rates however, because they tend to use faster and more lethal methods, such as hanging. Females tend to use overdoses, but their methods are becoming more lethal.

Recognise the symptoms of depression

Whenever a child feels miserable and bad about themselves for much of the time, and has lost interest in the things that they normally enjoy, then they are clinically depressed. There are several symptoms used to diagnose depression, and most people suffering from depression will have at least five or six. Females tend to experience more symptoms than males.

They –

- feel unhappy most of the time – but may feel a little better in the evenings
- experience depressed mood
- lose interest in life and can't enjoy anything
- lose their appetite or can't stop eating, so they may lose weight or keep putting on weight

- lose their self-confidence
- find it harder to make decisions
- feel agitated and restless – or lethargic
- have trouble sleeping – or feel the need to sleep all the time
- can't cope with things they used to
- feel useless, inadequate and hopeless
- have very low energy
- have feelings of worthlessness or guilt
- have difficulties in thinking
- have difficulty concentrating, staying focused and completing tasks
- avoid other people
- feel irritable
- if they are old enough to have sexual feelings, (they) lose interest in sex
- feel worse at a particular time each day, usually in the morning
- have recurrent thoughts of death or suicide

What to do if you think your child is already depressed or suicidal

Turn to the final section of the book, *Protecting a depressed or suicidal child*, for a systematic strategy. This section is immediately before the conclusion.

Right up front, let me stress two points.

First, if you think a child may be depressed already, take them to a good doctor, counsellor or psychologist straight away for

a careful diagnosis. Early diagnosis and treatment is crucially important in stopping depression taking hold. You can use the strategies in this book to help you identify and remove specific causes of their depression, and directly increase their joy and personal power to create a more satisfying life.

Second, if you think a child may be suicidal, act immediately. Ask them gently but directly if they are feeling suicidal. They will usually tell you. Listen carefully and non-judgementally to what they say. Then, if they are feeling suicidal, act immediately. Talk to at least two health care professionals who are good in this area and recommended by people you trust. Get help to find a key carer, create an intervention plan and organise three support teams.

The strategies and knowledge contained in this book will help you restore and strengthen well-being in children who are depressed or suicidal.

Protecting children from depression

Our broad goal is to build happiness and keep the naturally occurring periods of depression as short and easily resolved as possible, while at the same time letting the insights, mutual compassion and bonds of sympathy form between people.

This success relies on the dynamic skills, morale and conscious, loving wisdom of the groups to which each individual belongs, as well as the person's own personal morale and wisdom. Parents, teachers and counsellors have great power to increase the skills, morale and wisdom in their families, schools and communities. The primary function of this book is to help you achieve this.

Schools and teachers are all now in the well-being business in partnership with children and their parents. Teachers need to build well-being into daily school activities.

Counsellors, doctors and other healthcare professionals need to help children and their families create and strengthen their well-being, not simply treat the anxiety and depression, and certainly not simply see bad behaviour as something to expel or contain. Of course teachers and counsellors are not well-being experts, and neither are parents. Wisdom unfortunately is not sexually transmitted. So this new challenge which we all face, becoming well-being workers – wisdom workers rather than knowledge workers – is about trying more stuff, creating and exploring together, experimenting with different ideas and watching what happens.

It is vital that children are involved directly in these conversations and experiments to create well-being. In particular, it is very important that children are enabled to work together to build other people's well-being, rather than just their own. Not only is this a central moral principle and a source of social bonding and social capital – it creates changes to brain chemistry which increase happiness and motivation! Don't you love it when a plan comes together? In 2007, researchers at America's National Institute of Neurological Disorders and Stroke found that when people were generous to others – especially at a cost to themselves – their brains released the "pleasure chemical", dopamine, which increases desire and motivation. These acts of generosity also caused the brain to produce oxytocin, the "cuddle hormone", which is associated with forming strong attachments. None of this was caused by the givers thinking they would get a pat on the back – their generous acts were anonymous. Oxytocin not only increases trust, it increases a major component of emotional intelligence, the ability to recognise emotions in others from their body language. *New Scientist* magazine, 17 March 2007, reported that researchers at Rostock University in Germany had established that men exposed to the hormone were significantly better at emotional recognition.

This book brings together current scientific knowledge and strategies which you can apply where you are, at home or in a school, or in a community. It also offers parents many practical ideas.

It is important to remember that families, schools and communities are small, and this means that you as an individual, or as a member of a very small group, have surprising power to enrich the family culture and the make the school and community culture more engaging and friendly for children.

Well-being work is fun

You have many ways to empower children to create happiness and well-being for themselves and others. This work is much more fun for everyone than you may now imagine. It brings out wonderful creativity and synergy – and builds friendships and networks across divides of age, faith, income and occupation. You will learn the enduring strength of what Robert Putnam calls weak horizontal ties – those friendships which are formed when people come together briefly to share an important or enjoyable activity – and the miraculous spans of what he calls bridging capital – the bonds of mutual affection and understanding which form between different groups when they cooperate to serve the greater good.

WHY IS IT SO IMPORTANT TO PREVENT DEPRESSION?

Because clinical depression is dangerous ...

➢ It increases the risk of suicide

➢ It causes damaging changes to brain structures and brain development

➢ Depression changes people's ability to perceive, to think, to remember, to learn and to function, and yet often they are completely unaware of these negative changes

➢ It is often difficult to treat

➢ Drugs don't always work

➢ Drugs can cause a range of dangerous effects, particularly in children

➢ Depression often recurs

➢ Depression increases the risk of alcohol and drug abuse, as attempts at self-medication, drowning sorrows, getting out of it, etc

➢ Depression can have life-damaging consequences on children's education, careers, relationships and social integration

You can take many simple, effective actions which will help prevent children from developing depression. This is called primary prevention. More than that, if you work together with other parents, you can help each other and significantly reduce the risk of all your children falling victim to this epidemic of depression which is sweeping the world.

But you do not want your children to become depressed! Depression is like a car accident or an accident in the workplace. It is always better to prevent the accident in the first place than have any amount of high-quality treatment afterwards. Similarly, its treatment may involve several specialists, but its prevention does not. Preventing depression involves improving the social fabric around your children. Primary prevention of depression is about changing the social structures and practices which carry your children through their childhood, so that they do not develop depression. You want them to thrive – to be joyful and full of life.

So what can you do?

What actions can help you prevent depression in these children that you treasure?

The answer is that there are many simple actions which you can take to help protect your children from depression.

All these actions fit into a framework of seven strategies. These strategies are based on recent scientific research and have been developed from the award-winning Australian Youth Suicide Prevention Project – Project X – which I managed. They will give you a clear and integrated plan with tools you can put into practice today.

I will list them first, and then explore them one by one.

Seven Strategies for preventing depression

Strategy 1: Understanding depression

Strategy 2: Understanding the five elements of human well-being

Strategy 3: Increasing the flow of joy

Strategy 4: Increasing the flow of love and connection

Strategy 5: Organising the transmission of wisdom

Strategy 6: Empowering children

Strategy 7: Building morale

Understanding depression

This chapter gives you five different perspectives to help you understand depression.

1 the social foundations of depression

2 the biochemical foundations of depression

3 the evolutionary foundations of depression – the surprising benefits of depression

4 understanding the experience of depression – why depression feels so bad

5 how depression is ended naturally – emotional homeostasis and the sympathy group

1 The social foundations of depression

Pukapuka is a tiny Polynesian island in the South Pacific. There are around 600 children living on the island. For four years in the 1980s, Dr Steve Kinnear was the island doctor. In that time he saw one teenager with mild depression. By contrast, in Australia, the 2006 report of the New South Wales Chief Health Officer found that 20% of schoolgirls were experiencing psychological distress. In the same year in Western Australia, a study by the Queen Elizabeth Medical Centre

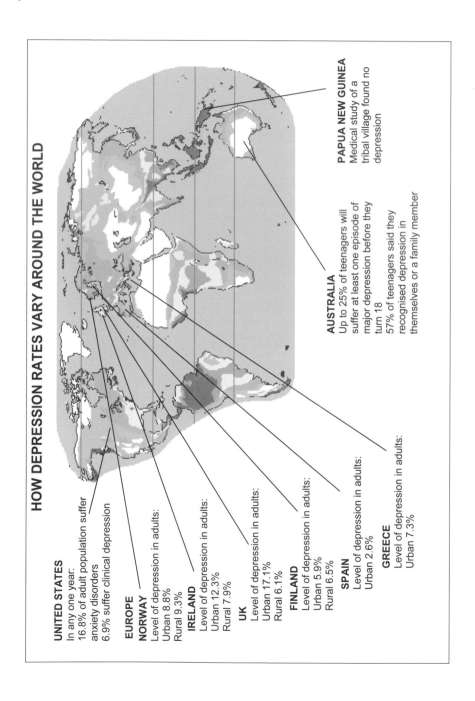

HOW DEPRESSION RATES VARY AROUND THE WORLD

UNITED STATES
In any one year:
16.8% of adult population suffer
anxiety disorders
6.9% suffer clinical depression

EUROPE
NORWAY
Level of depression in adults:
Urban 8.8%
Rural 9.3%

IRELAND
Level of depression in adults:
Urban 12.3%
Rural 7.9%

UK
Level of depression in adults:
Urban 17.1%
Rural 6.1%

FINLAND
Level of depression in adults:
Urban 5.9%
Rural 6.5%

SPAIN
Level of depression in adults:
Urban 2.6%

GREECE
Level of depression in adults:
Urban 7.3%

AUSTRALIA
Up to 25% of teenagers will
suffer at least one episode of
major depression before they
turn 18
57% of teenagers said they
recognised depression in
themselves or a family member

PAPUA NEW GUINEA
Medical study of a
tribal village found no
depression

found that 32% of 9 to 12-year-olds were either depressed or vulnerable to depression.

The single most intriguing feature of depression is how much it varies between groups. In groups where individuals feel easily included and valued – and their feelings are accepted with sympathy and understanding – rates of depression are low.

The central fact about depression is that it is sociobiological – a social fact: different social groups generate quite distinct and different rates of depression. Furthermore, these distinct rates of depression tend to remain stable over time unless there is specific social change in the group.

For example, in 1999, the World Health Organization published a study of depression rates across Europe. It showed that a person living in London was six times more likely to suffer depression than a person living in Madrid. A person living in Helsinki was twice as likely to be depressed as someone in Madrid, but had only a third the risk of depression of a resident of London. Why is there this huge variation? It is clearly not related to incomes or unemployment rates, since London has the highest per capita income of the three cities, and a similar unemployment rate. It is not simply due to massive variations in individual psychology – no one claims that people in London are six times more distorted in their thinking than people in Madrid.

Two key differences between cultures – social integration and moral regulation

The wide variation in rates of depression is caused by differences in the cultures of these different communities. In particular, there are two key qualities which vary between different cultural groups: the first quality is the degree of social integration, and the second quality is the degree of moral regulation. It is important for people, particularly children, to have the right amount of social integration and moral regulation – not too little and not too much. Too much destroys individual freedom, initiative and power, while too little creates anxiety, loneliness and loss of trust.

Social integration is a measure of how intimately and widely each person is connected to their community and social group. It includes not merely the number of friendships, roles and relationships, but how often each person sees these people, and the strength of these bonds.

Too little social integration or loss of physical contact can cause anxiety and depression. For example, when older people are suddenly physically isolated by breaking a hip, they can become clinically depressed quite unexpectedly, simply because they don't see their friends for a short while.

Too much social integration can cause depression because the person loses their individuality and power to make choices for themselves. Postnatal depression is so powerful because new mothers lose lots of their previous relationships, roles and connections, and at the same time, are forced into an overwhelming degree of social integration with the new baby, where they lose their freedom and their power to make choices for themselves.

Moral regulation is a measure of how well the group knows what its values and beliefs are – and how well it teaches and practices these values and beliefs. The most shocking collapses in mental health occur when these values and beliefs are destroyed by progress or by defeat and colonisation.

To illustrate this, let's take two examples.

The world's highest rates of attempted suicide occur in aboriginal Australians, where their complex culture was vigorously destroyed by white settlers. Their own moral regulation was suppressed and punished by Christian missionaries into the 1970s, and then comprehensively debilitated by the effects of passive welfare – "sit-down money"   and high alcohol consumption.

In Russia, the life expectancy of Russian men has dropped since 1989. Researchers at the National Centre for Preventive Medicine conducted a study, published in the book *Why Russians Are Becoming Extinct*, suggesting that the drop in life expectancy was due to the sudden change in values and morals as Russia switched to a consumer society.

Confusion, despair and anomie – the loss of norms and values – drive up levels of depression and aggression when there is too little moral regulation. When there is too much moral regulation, depression and suicide rates also increase – as do honour killings.

Children are particularly vulnerable to poor social integration. They have little power to visit family and friends, or to create satisfying social gatherings. School itself is designed to separate children from adults and to prevent children of different ages working and playing together. Instead, it forces children of the same age together – which brings out their most competitive attitudes and behaviour, rather than the easier friendships, greater helpfulness and uncompetitive mutual respect which can happen more readily between older and younger people.

Children are also very vulnerable to failures of moral regulation in their social group or their community. When social values collapse, those who are more powerful bully and exploit those who are weaker, and the rise of bullying is now a feature of schools and street culture in many countries.

The vital role of elders

Social integration and moral regulation are organised and maintained by the elders in any group. The elders are those people, such as parents, grandparents, uncles and aunts, teachers, etc, who take responsibility for nurturing the well-being of the group.

When elders work together over time, sharing their perceptions and creativity, this combination of social integration and moral regulation creates collective consciousness and a collective conscience. The group notices itself, and notices the relationships and well-being needs of each member, and the group cares for itself – the collective conscience is not a burden but a learnt desire to look after each person's well-being.

Stable traditional cultures provide extraordinary protection from stress and depression for both children and adults. These cultures do not eliminate aggression and competition – rather, they incorporate competition into rituals and celebrations which honour winners and losers alike. Probably the most famous example are the Nubian wrestlers.

For thousands of years, Nubian tribes have lived in the regions of Sudan south of the fourth cataract of the Nile River. They survive by herding cattle, and wrestling in the cattle camps is the central sport of the tribe, as well as the main activity by which character, skills and leadership are developed.

Through this wrestling, the young men are initiated into manhood, learn to endure pain, work hard, and be courageous. They learn how to be defeated without becoming depressed, how to win without becoming vain or cruel, how to build unity and well-being out of these fierce contests.

There is a strong spiritual and moral dimension to this cultural training. The strength and prowess enable the young men to care for the herd and their village. The training consciously links them to the spirits of all living things, to their ancestors and to life's essence – represented by the ash of burnt trees, which they use to decorate their bodies. They learn to meditate together to see the profoundness of life and realise the depth and value of their fraternity and culture. These Nubian tribes are famous for their fierce, dynamic vitality.

Progress undermines elders

Aggression and depression are two sides of the same coin. Any loss of moral regulation, producing a small increase in visible aggression, such as bullying, or street assaults, carried out by a small number of children and youth, produces a much larger increase in stress, anxiety and depression in the whole population of children.

Part of this general stress comes from the sense that the whole group doesn't care enough to pay attention, protect the weak and innocent, and enforce fairness and respect. Children learn helplessness and develop strong negative beliefs about themselves and their relationships with others – which are widely recognised to be the psychological roots of depression.

Progress,(as we shall see later) ironically destroys people's confidence in their values and in their right to teach and enforce them. The elders become silent and isolated. They lose their shared attentiveness and the organising principles by which they nurture well-being in their families and community. The group becomes unconscious.

Again, children are very vulnerable, because elders stop watching and shaping their well-being, and stop having the confidence to know how to meet their emotional needs, their need for wisdom and their need for a sense of meaning, purpose and morale.

Children rely very much on loving interactions with their elders to give them their sense of belonging and worth, and they rely on elders to create the opportunities to let them build their own groups of sympathetic friends. Psychologists call these sympathy groups – where friends provide each other with encouragement, understanding, advice and help, excitement and commiseration. Sharing experiences and feelings builds empathy, and social and emotional intelligence. This sharing is the key to rebalancing emotions – social emotional homeostasis – the foundation of resilience.

To get a picture of how depression is a social fact, imagine a trampoline. A whole group of springs are connected by a strong woven fabric. They are each also attached to a rigid steel frame. When you jump on a trampoline the flexible fabric shares your load among all the springs. No single spring gets overstretched.

So, in a strong social group each burden is distributed equally by the fabric of connections. The rigid framework is the shared moral code and learnt of principles of the group.

Both the fabric of connections and the moral framework are created and maintained by the active wisdom of the group, particularly by parents and other elders. It takes a lot of time and skill, conversations and creativity for a community to achieve that vital balance of social integration and moral regulation which nurture well-being and prevent children (and adults) developing depression.

2 The biochemical foundations of depression – the role of the brain in depression

Now we have looked at some of the social and cultural elements which underlie depression, it is necessary to explore some of the biology of depression, because depression is fundamentally sociobiological – the social conditions around each child powerfully affect their thoughts and feelings, which in turn affect the chemistry and then the structures of their brain. We could call this the sociobiochemistry of depression.

Depression, as it occurs in the brain, is a complex, progressive condition.

The brain

It is worth understanding something of the human brain because our social relationships and our thoughts directly and continuously change our brain chemistry, which changes our mood. The first section of the appendix at the back of this book sets out some more basic brain facts, and includes diagrams to give you more details of the structures of the brain.

It has intense sensitivity to social relationships. The core of stress is loss, loss of social status, relationship or security. When we lose status or lose physical contact with our friends, we almost automatically become depressed. We are designed by evolution to live in a stable social group of about 150, and to have a sympathy group of around 8 to 15 closer friends.

Thinking and feeling combine, so that we "add up" our conclusions far more by how we feel, than by using logic without any emotion. As well, our moods alter our thoughts, which then in turn trigger further altered emotions and moods.

This is why it is important for children to learn optimism. Then their self-confidence and optimistic mood help them think more effectively and creatively to solve any problems which threaten their well-being. This builds resilience – and also makes them feel much more relaxed about asking other people to help when they need them. This in turn builds their sense of prowess and morale.

Conversely, it is why depression entrenches itself: when people feel hopeless, their thinking becomes more pessimistic, less creative and less effective, so that they fail to solve their problems. They tend, then, to draw general conclusions which are disempowering, distorted – and depressing. They lose self-esteem and withdraw – and don't ask for help just when they need it most. They lose their sense of morale.

Thinking and feeling are controlled by brain chemicals, neurotransmitters, and, to make it complicated, these brain chemicals are in turn controlled by thinking and feeling. We have over 100 different neurotransmitters. When our thoughts and feelings become predominantly negative or when we are stressed for more than two weeks continuously, our nerve cells are damaged by these powerful chemicals and our brain changes its structures to adapt to the changed levels of these brain chemicals.

Why children need sleep

The brain only keeps tiny quantities of these neurotransmitters, and makes new quantities while we sleep. Stress, long periods of work or intense emotion, certain drugs, or lack of sleep can exhaust the brain supplies of important neurotransmitters. We experience this as depression – and this depression can be so intense that we become suicidal.

This is why we have to limit the demands we place on children to continuously increase their educational efforts, and why we must resist their own demands to swap sleep for late-night stimulations such as television, computer and electronic games. It is also why binge drinking and party drugs such as cocaine, ecstasy and speed are so dangerous for children.

Dopamine and serotonin are rather like oil in an engine – without them the brain will not run smoothly, and damages itself. In a remarkable study in 1999 at the New York State Psychiatric Institute, researchers examined sections of the brains taken from people who had committed suicide. Under the microscope, the researchers discovered that the prefrontal cortex had lost crucial serotonin transporter neurons, and the gland which makes and supplies this serotonin had altered in an unsuccessful attempt to produce more.

Why children need friends

We naturally use conversations and sympathy to rebalance our emotions and restore our neurotransmitter levels. Maintaining this balance is as important to our mental health as maintaining our body temperature is to our physical health. If we do not provide children with the friendships and opportunities for this social-emotional homeostasis, then negative emotions can accumulate, creating pessimistic and distorted self talk, producing imbalances in neurotransmitter levels which turn into self-perpetuating depression.

The human brain is particularly tuned to respond to any change in the social context. Even tiny changes can produce huge changes in these neurotransmitter mixtures.

For example, a contemptuous glance of half a second from a peer can flood us with rage or shame or despair. On the other hand, a tiny half-smile from a close friend can instantly melt our tension and restore confidence – and a tiny half-smile from someone we desire can flood us with joy. No doubt you can remember the speed and power of these sudden feelings in yourself – the subjective experiences of surges in neurotransmitter levels which may take less than a 30th of a second to occur.

Children, and particularly girls, can give meanings to these often ambiguous interactions so fast and so unconsciously that the power of these emotional reactions confuses them and leaves them drained at the end of every day. It is possible to become depressed simply through a combination of great sensitivity and great imagination, where there are no calm, wise, loving voices to help children share their powerful thoughts and feelings and make sense of them.

Why depression has two distinctly different stages

As I explained in the introduction, there is naturally occurring short-term depression, and then there is longer-term clinical depression. We can now look at how this occurs in the brain.

We can start with a simple analogy.

Imagine you have a steel spring made of a coil of fine wire, and it's hanging from a strong hook in your ceiling. Now imagine you are holding the lower end of the spring in your hands, and you start to pull down on the spring. As you pull harder, the spring stretches further. You can feel it pulling against you. You relax your force and the spring pulls itself up back to its original length.

This is like the first stage of depression. When you are not under any strain or burden your spirits are naturally buoyant and a little high – your natural happiness. Any stress or threat pulls your spirits down. As the stress lifts and the threat recedes, so your spirits lift, and your good mood returns.

Now imagine you are pulling down on the spring again. This time, you put all your weight on the thin spring. For a while, it stretches evenly, as before. But then you pull it past the limit of its elasticity. It deforms. Some of the coils straighten out. Now you release it, but it cannot pull itself back to its original shape. It hangs low permanently.

This is like the second stage of depression. Depression becomes an illness whenever a person's spirits and mood cannot rise naturally to their normal high level. This second stage, clinical depression, requires prompt medical or psychological treatment, just like any other illness or disease. Just as the overstretched spring cannot pull itself together, neither can a person with clinical depression pull themselves together, no matter how much you or they want to. The trouble is, while you can see at a glance that the spring is damaged, you cannot see the damage in a person with clinical depression.

So how do these two stages of depression happen in the brain?

Very simply, in the first stage, when we feel stressed or lose status, our neurotransmitter levels change.

In the second stage, these changed levels of chemicals cause changes to our brain structures.

In the first stage, if we feel stressed or anxious our body responds by increasing three important neurotransmitters. It produces higher levels of cortisol, the powerful stress hormone, higher levels of norepinephrine, a neurotransmitter which makes us focus our attention, and higher levels of dopamine, the neurotransmitter responsible for motivation.

This makes us very focused, motivated and aroused to confront or escape from the threat to our well-being. It makes us very serious, because one of the effects of cortisol is to cause the brain to reduce levels of serotonin, the neurotransmitter most responsible for lifting our mood. If you are confronted by a snake, or see your child about to drown, it is vital that you become instantly serious and focused.

However, two things happen if the stress continues, if it is overwhelming and beyond your power to defeat.

First, you exhaust your small supplies of dopamine, norepinephrine and serotonin -- but not your supplies of cortisol, which is created in huge glands attached to the kidneys. You may then feel extremely anxious, agitated but exhausted. You feel at the same time depressed and yet mentally hyperactive, trapped and yet unable to focus and without the drive to apply your willpower and effort to escape or resolve the threat to your well-being.

How stress damages children's brains

Second, your brain begins to be damaged by these altered levels of neurotransmitters and cortisol. Both cortisol and another neurotransmitter, glutamate, which the brain releases in large quantities under stress, start to damage and kill nerve cells in the brain. The two parts of the brain most readily damaged are the left and right hippocampus -- which are very important in creating and consolidating memories. The underneath of each hippocampus contains an area called the dentate gyrus, which is where new brain cells are produced.

Cortisol and glutamate destroy these new brain cells as well. Brain scans and autopsies of people with severe depression revealed shrunken hippocampuses, including much smaller dentate gyruses.

Antidepressant medications work not just because they stop the brain getting rid of serotonin and norepinephrine, but also because they increase the brain chemicals which help repair injured nerve cells and promote the growth of new ones – particularly in each hippocampus and dentate gyrus.

Physical exercise also counters clinical depression by building new brain cells in the dentate gyrus. In a study led by Dr Scott Small, at Columbia University Medical Centre in New York, and reported by Reuters in March 2007, it was discovered that exercise increased blood flow to the dentate gyrus, stimulating the growth of new brain cells, and, as fitness increased, so did blood flow.

Four ways to protect the brain from depression

By understanding these features of the brain, we can immediately see four ways to protect against depression:

1 Increase sleep. Insist on regular sensible bedtimes and keep television, video games and computers out of the bedroom. Even very small amounts of sleep deprivation provoke an immune system reaction, and produce higher levels of cortisol. Sleep not only strengthens memory and replenishes neurotransmitters, it also helps people extract meanings, themes and generalised rules from what they have learnt during the day.

2 Avoid stress. Break unavoidable stresses into short periods, so that the brain has time to get rid of excess cortisol and glutamate, and restore serotonin and dopamine levels.

3 Increase exercise and build fitness. One of the most important activities to counter depression is playing team sports in the evenings. This not only builds fitness – it also builds valuable friendships, increases morale and releases endorphins – the brain's most powerful feel-good chemicals.

4 Increase the time children spend honestly sharing their experiences and feelings with their close friends, and listening with active sympathy and encouragement to each other's stories and feelings. Feeling heard discharges emotions and restores calmness and self-esteem.

3 The evolutionary foundations of depression – the surprising benefits of depression

The deep, evolutionary foundation of depression is not a mystery. It is not something new or specific to humans. All mammals are able to be depressed, even very small ones like mice.

Depression is a naturally occurring behaviour built into our genetic design. Furthermore, it plays a very important part in our evolutionary success. This may sound strange or cruel, but once you understand the role of depression, then you will be able to prevent it from getting out of hand.

The dynamic process of human evolution and organisation is based on violent collisions, dominance contests. They are not avoidable – they lie at the heart of human evolution and they provoke our most powerful interactions and emotions.

Humans are a species of socially organised, predacious primate. We are particularly dangerous predators because we are omnivorous, but we're not like any other omnivores.

Because of the extraordinary development of our intelligence, language and powers of mental association, we are symbolic omnivores. We hunt and consume things because of their meaning, such as shark fins, larks' tongues, new cars, new clothes, etc – anything that takes our fancy. We can desire and consume a city or a country as easily as blackbirds consume worms.

This means that there are no limits to our appetites – and there are no limits to the range and frequency of our competitions for dominance. Whatever we have we can naturally want more of. Whatever anybody else has which we think is valuable, we tend to want for ourselves. Humans therefore have far more things to compete over than other species.

Humans also have a far greater range of skills and abilities than other species, and we invent new ones all the time, so we have far more ways to compete. No other species competes over tennis or golf. No other species competes over general knowledge, plays crosswords or trivial pursuit. No other species has developed over 1000 new computer games in the last three years.

Humans also have much more power to change or destroy their environment and their social fabric than other species. When people lose their home or their community, then they have to go through a whole new array of dominance contests to create the new social fabric and find their proper place in it – their status.

These facts mean that humans are subject to far more frequent and complicated dominance contests than other species. So we create much more stress and anxiety – and more depression, because it is very common that status is under threat – and there are always several things we're not very good at.

<u>Biological Design Envelope</u>

1.   We are designed to live in a stable social group of 148 people.

2.   We are designed to have a stable sympathy group of 8-15 friends.

3.   We are designed to spend 4-6 hours each day in social grooming with friends.

4.   We are designed to feel stress whenever our social status in our social group is under threat.

5.   We are designed to develop by free physical play with others of all ages.

6.   We are designed to feel compassion and sympathy and to help each other rebalance emotionally – **social homeostasis.**

Paradoxically, the more a child excels, and the more they are a brilliant allrounder, the more likely they are to feel insecure and incompetent – because their elevated vision may simply show them unwinnable dominance contests stretching out in every direction. Each year newspapers tell stories of children and young adults committing suicide despite their high intelligence, high achievements and many friends.

How much we get is determined by the power of our social group and our status in our group. Each group puts pressure on itself and its members – particularly its children – to increase its competitive power, protect itself and capture more territory and wealth.

Human status is inherently vulnerable. Human groups are even more inherently unstable and vulnerable. For over two million years, we have hunted other human groups, and been hunted by them. There is no other species which so ruthlessly and persistently preys upon its own kind. Like all primates, we survive individually only because of our social organisation, and human social organisation is always a dominance hierarchy.

Our brains are designed for social organization – including dominance contests and defeat – but we have a design envelope.

Robin Dunbar, the British ethnobiologist, established that humans are genetically designed to live in a stable social group of 148 members, and to have a close group, the sympathy group, of eight to fifteen people, within that social group. The main actions of individuals within each social group are cooperative, but cooperation and sharing is very unequal, according to status.

Every social group is under the control of a dominant leader or leadership group. It is vital for the evolutionary success of the group that the leader is always the most dominant among the group and that group members develop and test their power. A weak or ageing leader threatens the survival of the whole group.

So there must be a dynamic process which allows dominance contests. Each competitor must be able to use their full power and intelligence. The dominance contest has to be a violent collision. It has to be violent enough to break the bonds of dominance. But equally, the dominance contest should not kill or seriously injure the antagonists. This would dangerously weaken the group.

This is where the genetic design of primate and human biochemistry plays a part. Aggression and depression fit together. Whenever humans enter a dominance contest, their brains release the powerful stress hormones to pump them up for maximum power. This is the fight or flight mechanism. Both antagonists are able to fight as hard as they can. They fight until dominance is established. Our brains are designed to recognize defeat, and so when we see that our position is hopeless, we despair and we feel defeated; our energy and our morale collapse.

As soon as the dominant individual has defeated the weaker one, the brain chemistry changes rapidly. The winner's brain increases the supply of serotonin. Serotonin is the neurotransmitter which primarily controls mood. So the winner feels good. (Who said that "Winners are grinners" ?) Their mental functioning is increased. The loser's brain reduces the supply of serotonin, and the loser feels depressed. So the loser withdraws and loses motivation and power.

Can you see what this does? It protects both the winner and the loser by stopping the will to fight, immediately dominance has been established. Importantly, it stops the loser from continuing to antagonise the more powerful winner – which might drive the winner to kill or maim the loser. When the loser shows that they submit and admit that they are defeated, the mood of the winner immediately changes from enraged aggression to peaceful superiority – the emotions of triumph often include feelings of generosity and general goodwill – magnanimity.

When a new dominant leader has triumphed, then they reorganise the group, with new bonds forming a new structure. This process is very similar to any chemical reaction. The defeated and biochemically subdued – depressed – loser fits into the new structure in a position determined by their new value and bonding power.

The main reason for the global dominance of democracies is because they make these dominance competitions very efficient and safe. New leaders can quickly rise to the top if they are indeed the best; parties can continuously reorganise their elected members to best use the relative strengths of each person; voters can regularly choose the best party to form government. Losers are honoured, inevitably given less valuable roles, and encouraged to learn from every defeat, develop their powers and try again next time.

At the same time, the huge rise in depression rates – particularly childhood depression rates – in these very successful democracies is caused by a huge increase in the pressure to compete in dominance contests. This competitive pressure between democracies is the main driver of progress, and the competition between individuals drives up their productivity, which, collectively, raises the economic and educational performance of the nation.

At the same time that we have ignored the ecological destruction caused by this endless race for progress and competitive advantage, we have ignored the social destruction which has radically changed the whole basis of status and security for children.

Experiments carried out on several primate species show that loss of status results in lowered serotonin levels. Probably the major reason why females have higher levels of depression than males is because humans are a species – like many others – where males tend generally to seek to dominate females. It requires a continuous political, cultural and economic struggle to resist this innate tendency, which is incorporated into every culture and every religion.

Progress, stress and the costs of status

Progress is driven by competition between groups. Progress is a process of increasing the rate of change -- which means increasing instability in every human group. Progress means that we make more products and we make each product more complicated, with more features but costing more. Work becomes more difficult and we need more products to feel that we are keeping our place in the group.

Competition between groups, particularly between nations, is increasing. As our society becomes less stable, we experience more stress because we automatically face more dominance contests, and our sympathy groups are weaker. The groups we belong to change much faster, so our status decays or simply dissipates. When we add cultural change to this, our stress increases much more because no-one can tell us what the rules are for moral regulation and how dominance should be contested in order to protect the weak.

The most important causal factor in depression is **chronic stress** leading to strong negative beliefs about yourself and your relationship with others. Human stress is overwhelmingly about threats to individual social status and control.

The two kinds of status

So let's look at **status** – our place or our rank in our social group. There are two kinds of status – two different ways we get status and connection. The first is **automatic status**, given to us by a group just for belonging to it. Automatic status is created and given by elders. The second is **performance status**, which we have to earn by our achievements or win by competing against other group members.

Automatic status is very important for children and for adults because it is not stressful, it is stable and secure, and it cannot be taken from us by anyone stronger or smarter or richer. In a good family, and in a close community, a baby is cherished just because it has been born. The child doesn't have to do anything it has status automatically. Automatic status gives children a natural sense of security, identity and confidence. It sets them free to be themselves and be loved and included, just for being who they are. Automatic status means that you are valued, you are noticed, the group cares about your emotional states and well-being.

Automatic status also gives children strength and protection

THE DIFFERENCE THAT AUTOMATIC STATUS MAKES

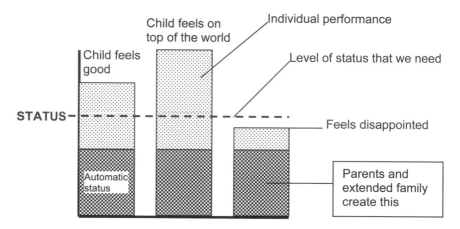

1.   High level of automatic status
   Child feels loved, secure, connected

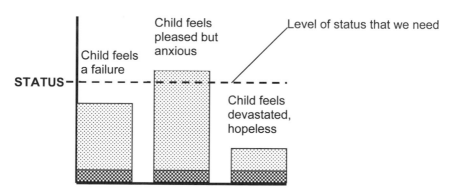

2.   Low level of automatic status
   Child feels chronic stress, anxiety, on edge

from stress and depression because, like the springs in the trampoline, they are connected to the other group members who love and value them automatically and will share their load. But now, right across the world, automatic status and connection is rapidly decreasing. Our families and communities are getting smaller and getting weaker, less stable and less enduring. At the same time schools are getting bigger and less personal, but with higher turnover of staff and students, and more demands to perform – the worst possible combination for creating a sense of belonging and giving children worthwhile automatic status. The individuality of each child is a potential menace, a threat and a problem to the smooth running of an impersonal educational bureaucracy.

As the amount of face-to-face interaction shrinks, people can't make these fundamental social bonds. The face-to-face interaction at school narrows in scope to mainly prepare for educational contests and administer them. Many children now don't feel like they belong to any social group and don't have any sympathy group. It takes time to form human bonds, and you need to be able to easily get together often and feel free to just talk and play together and do stuff.

If your children don't know their neighbours and the members of their local community, they are likely to feel rejected – judged, feared and ignored. The neighbourhood becomes **socially toxic.**

There is a massive shift in the basis of our status, especially for children, because they have so little power and freedom to choose what they do and who they see. The shift is away from automatic status to performance status.

Performance status is a constant pressure. You are always vulnerable since your performance can slip or someone else can do better. Also, the rules are always tricky. So what if you are kind and work hard? I've got a better body and more expensive shoes! So what if you got 85% for maths on Friday? Today is Monday and there's a new test, on new stuff – you're still at risk – only more so if you did well last time. You can get a credit and still lose your reputation.

This is one reason why bright, hardworking students can easily become depressed. Many suicides are brilliant and successful young people, who had been, in fact, envied by their peers.

The competition between nations means that governments put pressure on schools to increase educational outcomes. At the same time, because of the rising costs and difficulties of keeping up with progress, parents also put pressure on schools to increase the educational outcomes their children achieve. It's not enough for children to simply go to school – and get automatic status. Teachers are under pressure to put students under pressure to make them care very much about how hard they work and how good their results are – performance status is all that is offered, all that counts.

The more our status is based on performance, the more stress we feel, and children are particularly vulnerable. We are acutely sensitive to our social context, so as the norms and atmosphere become more competitive, we are much more likely to feel anxious. Also, because there is never any safe endpoint to educational competition and to the negative attitudes which continual competition provokes in children, they are much more likely to form strong negative beliefs about their own worth and abilities, and about their relationships. These beliefs are not deluded or distorted: they are in most cases completely accurate generalisations formed from their experiences at school.

When people are focused on competing for performance status, they actively dislike cooperating or helping, and they don't have time or desire to really make friends and maintain sympathy groups.

But performance status is a treadmill. It is endlessly repetitive and stressful because as soon as one success is achieved, it is past and the status fades. This creates stress and the stress creates an inability to cope with your own emotions, and a tendency to be irritated or overwhelmed by the feelings of others.

Think about what gives your children their sense of status and belonging. You have the creative power to boost their status and make it more secure.

4 Understanding the experience of depression – why depression feels so bad

There are three key features of the experience of depression which make it the most dangerous illness;

> 1 – hopelessness
>
> 2 – a barrier
>
> 3 – mental agony

These three features can combine to make death seem the most attractive option. They can produce a continuous craving for intoxication or extreme risktaking as a way of breaking free or shutting out the mental pain.

Hopelessness

The hopelessness and sense of despair are often accompanied by a sense of fatalism, passivity and cynicism, which make it very difficult for a depressed person to make any sustained positive action, or believe that things can change.

A barrier

The barrier is described by the clinical psychologist, Dorothy Rowe, as the fundamental difference between unhappiness and depression. She said that, "When you are depressed, you feel that there is an invisible barrier between you and the rest of the world and nothing gets through that barrier. It is a prison. When we are unhappy, even if the most terrible things happen to us, we can be comforted. Someone who is depressed will actually move away from a hug because they don't want it. So it's a very distinctive feeling."

The American poet, Sylvia Plath, called her experience of this barrier *The Bell Jar*, in her book of the same name, a ground-breaking autobiographical novel about her manic depression. She was tragically unable to break out of her bell jar, and committed suicide after 10 years, in 1963.

The barrier is a profound sense of disconnection, producing feelings of detachment and estrangement. It becomes difficult for the depressed person to find any meaningful patterns or importance in their experiences – or in the concerns and efforts of their friends. This can be intensely irritating to the people who love and try to help the depressed person – they appear cut off, incredibly self-centred, needy but passive, determined to make no effort to help themselves.

Mental agony – why depression makes people want to die

Mental agony is the single most dangerous feature of depression. Agony is a word used to describe extreme and excruciating pain. The mental pain of depression can become so unbearable that death is the only painkiller strong enough to provide relief. The intensity of this mental agony can make the depressed person as desperate and unprincipled as a heroin addict – and just as hard to cure. They can abandon and betray everyone they love and lose sight of everything that previously they lived for.

You may have heard of the *Peter Principle*. Dr Laurence J. Peters proposed the principle that, in any hierarchy, people rise to their level of incompetence. His witty logical conclusion was that each position in any bureaucracy is therefore filled by an incompetent – because anyone who was still competent in the job would quickly be promoted to a more difficult job.

Depression occurs when we reach our level of incompetence – we are defeated by people or circumstances beyond our control.

Achievement = competence x effort

As we reach our level of incompetence we often increase our effort massively and panic as our achievement falls off.

For example, if our competence is effectively zero but we make a desperate, superhuman effort, our achievement is still at completely dreadful.

Achievement = 0% competence x (3 x normal) effort = 0

As the difficulty increases towards or past the level of incompetence, then anxiety increases and the levels of norepinephedrine and cortisol rise. The person begins to panic or feel under extreme stress – in mental agony. The word 'agony'

APPROACHING OUR LEVEL OF
INCOMPETENCE CAUSES AGONY

FREEDOM The goal and gift of wisdom	Wise elders - Loving action - Self realisation Self acceptance Peace, serenity Well-being is not limited to status but to the sacred well-being of the whole
ZONE OF TRANSFORMATION *It often takes a severe crisis before someone opens to the possibility of transformation*	Learn to attune inwards – to the self – the God within Learn to attune outwards – to the connectedness of all Transforming Personal growth required Wisdom or transforming social integration **LEVEL OF INCOMPETENCE**
ZONE OF AGONY Danger zone -brain neurotransmitters become depleted -depression, suicide -brain structures change	**LIMIT OF COMPETENCE** **More and more effort is required but we achieve less and less effect** Feelings of great distress, despair, panic or denial, depression
ZONE OF STRAIN	We have to push ourselves We feel our status is at risk **STRAIN** a sense of compelled stressful effort
ZONE OF MASTERY	We can gather the power to meet the challenges We can easily do the tasks Relaxed Confidence Play

RISING DIFFICULTY OF TASKS

comes from *agon* – the Greek word for the gladiator's place of combat – the quintessential dominance contest. We have a natural inclination to push our performance to our level of incompetence, where we can become trapped in this zone of mental agony.

At some point, a child or adult who feels driven to perform well beyond their level of competence can easily collapse into depression. Dopamine and norephinephrine supplies become exhausted but cortisol levels get even higher. Without strong fast social homeostasis, the depression becomes clinical – irreversible, and the cortisol starts to damage the hippocampus.

When your child's sense of **security, status and identity** are based on performance far more than on automatic status of belonging, then they are very vulnerable to the *Peter Principle*. A child can't create automatic status. Only the adult group can give it. And an unstable or unwise social group has almost no automatic status to give – like trying to borrow money from a bankrupt bank.

When a society or a social group is organized to make children continuously strain and compete against each other, as modern schools feel obliged to do, then many children live in the mental agony of always being publicly exposed at their level of incompetence.

How clinical depression causes competence to collapse

There is a tipping point between natural, short-term depression and clinical, long-term depression. It is not a gentle slide down into deeper unhappiness. After around two weeks, suddenly the experience of depression changes radically. Why?

The four main culprits are almost certainly the damage to the memory, neurotransmitter exhaustion, attention deficit trait, and the unwitting abandonment of the three activities which bring us happiness; frequently doing a variety of acts of kindness to others, consciously remembering to feel grateful, and choosing to be optimistic.

The damage to our ability to make and access memories has a powerful but completely unexpected consequence – our ability to imagine and create is also disabled. This means that our ability to think logically and to make plans – the way we manage our day-to-day living – suddenly becomes very difficult. We rely completely on the details of our memory to imagine choices, and we have to imagine choices before we can logically assess our options and make a plan. The more severe the depression, the more difficulty people have in remembering the details of their past or imagining a personal future.

Normally, we continuously create two kinds of memory, memories of facts and experiences, and memories of how we do things. These two kinds of memory are called declarative memory and procedural memory.

It is easy to see that we learn to be optimistic by continuously building our procedural memories of how to create and maintain our happiness and well-being. It is also easy to see that school pays almost no attention to helping children focus on developing these crucially useful personal memories.

This means that many children already have an invisible vulnerability – they are deficient in both their store of useful knowledge and in their habits of attention to create more of this knowledge each day. So once stress starts to damage short-term memory, their competence plummets, dragging down their confidence, self-esteem, even their sense of identity.

This experience can be every bit as humiliating as being stripped naked in public. Naturally, this triggers a protective withdrawal, which then, unfortunately also naturally, lowers their serotonin levels – and their mood falls even lower. Mental agony is a completely accurate description of how all this makes them feel.

The neurotransmitter exhaustion comes from struggling vainly to control a circumstance or problem which is too hard. We drain our biochemical batteries. We lose the ability to focus and motivate ourselves.

This produces a condition called attention deficit trait – very similar to ADHD. We are driven by fear, but are distracted, erratic, unable to focus, make decisions, or complete tasks. More Hell. More agony. More paralysis. We become so fatalistic and immobilised that we detach from our own struggle – the barrier descends. We are trapped in a Bell Jar. People can feel at the same time as though they are looking from the outside at an exhibit in a freak show – themselves.

From this completely negative mental state, it is very common for depressed people to downgrade all positives of their past, their friends and themselves. They create distorted thinking under the overwhelming pressure of their collapsed competence. It is as though the black sky has fallen on them, flattening and obliterating all familiar landmarks. This is why cognitive behavioural therapy is such a precise and potent tool, because it challenges each distortion with direct evidence.

If you can understand the experience of depression and imagine its emotional and cognitive power, then you can see why is so important to protect children from depression. Children need the comfort and wisdom of a strong and attentive group to teach them resilience, encourage and coach them, and restore their sense of worth and, with it, lift their spirits and their mood. They especially need to be protected from chronic stress.

Chronic stress is caused by high group demands, too many dominance contests, low social homeostasis or low social integration. The only other causes are wars, extreme poverty or debilitating injury or illness, and they do not account for the rising global epidemic of childhood depression.

This means that the root of this rising depression is poor or unwise leadership of social groups and of societies. Leaders and politicians are compromising and undermining the well-being of children in their drive to raise productivity and wealth – and it costs a lot of money to get psychiatrists for every family. As a result of these changes, fear, anxiety, stress and depression are rising in children in many countries: Britain, Japan, Australia, Germany, India, the United States, Singapore – the list goes on.

5 How depression is ended maturally – emotional homeostasis and the sympathy group

Homeostasis – how children restore emotional balance

We humans pride ourselves on our toughness and adaptability, but human well-being must be quite precisely maintained. If our temperature varies by more than a few degrees we are incapacitated by fever or hypothermia. If our blood sugar level varies by more than a small amount we go into shock. If we are depressed for more than two weeks then we cannot restore our emotional mood to normal. We are then clinically depressed and need skilled help, commonly counselling and medical treatment.

So how do children naturally end a period of depression and restore emotional equilibrium?

The answer is very simple – by individual and collective efforts. The individual works to recover, adapt and cheer up. The brain exerts its natural homeostasis – that is, it tries to rebalance itself, allowing the body to rest and the neurotransmitter levels to return to normal, restoring mood and motivation. At the same time that this individual homeostasis is under way, the primary social group, to which the individual belongs, notices their depressed mood and gives support and sympathy – social homeostasis. Across every culture, the most powerful social rituals are funerals. Everybody affected by the death comes together to share their grief, their sympathy and their love. The funeral is designed to help people release the depth of their suffering and rebalance their emotions. At a good funeral people move through the overwhelming feeling of grief to an

HOMEOSTASIS – how we respond to stress

TWO SEPARATE PATHWAYS

SOCIAL HOMEOSTASIS   **INDIVIDUAL HOMEOSTASIS**

	☺	☺	☺	☺	
☺	Group notices "That person is not OK" "So we are not OK until we restore their well-being"				☺
☺					☺
☺					☺
	☺			☺	

1. Stress reaction
2. Brain thinks of ways to defeat stress and restore well-being

SOCIAL	INDIVIDUAL
The group makes efforts to restore individual well-being Group decides to help the individual Group asks itself and the individual "What is the problem?" "What can we do?" Who has the parts of the solution?	3. Person makes efforts to restore well-being ▪ Seeks help perhaps ▪ Creates own ideas ▪ Works to achieve success ▪ Agonises over the duration of the stress

The group provides:
Sympathy - and - **Power**
*comfort   *physical assistance
*cheer   *resources
*consolation   *creative effort
*encouragement   *strategies
*understanding   *connections
Social homeostasis is limited by social integration and wisdom of groups
	Individual homeostasis is limited by
	▪ Isolation
	▪ Limits of own
	    *competence
	    *resilience
	▪ Brain biochemistry
	▪ Self-awareness

WELL-BEING IS BEST MAINTAINED WHEN BOTH SOCIAL AND INDIVIDUAL HOMEOSTASIS WORK TOGETHER

overwhelming feeling of love – and gratitude for that love.

This social homeostasis is vital in protecting mental health. It is primarily given by what psychologists have called **the sympathy group**.

So why do children need a sympathy group?

A sympathy group is the small group of people who really care about you, and whom you really care about. When one of the group is suffering or in trouble, the others feel sympathy automatically, and want to help and give sympathy, love and support.

All primates form sympathy groups. They groom each other, play and do things together and turn to each other for comfort or reassurance.

A healthy size for a human sympathy group is 8-15 individuals. Primates, for example chimpanzees, like to spend 4-6 hours each day hanging out with members of their sympathy group. In traditional hunter-gatherer societies, people spent a lot of each day in these informal groups, working and relaxing. A healthy social group is composed of these informal sympathy groups and the special group, the elders who watch over the well-being and interplay of the whole group.

Make sure you help your children to form their own sympathy groups and hang out with them.

The sympathy group is a core element in mental health and well-being.

First, it enhances, protects and restores the status of each member, maintaining their sense of worth and identity and belonging. The sympathy group shares its power and resources, creating synergy, new strategies and strong bonds of affection.

Second, the group enhances and restores the mood of each member. This is critical in lifting natural depression before it becomes an entrenched biochemical disorder.

Third, the group helps each person adapt to their changing life circumstances and grow wiser. Wisdom and other nutrients flow through the group to the person who is currently stressed or in need. The group draws on its memory and together co-creates or hunts for useful wisdom for each other.

Fourth, the group contributes to each individual's sense of morale and identity.

The big question then is how is depression lifted naturally, in ordinary community life?

How is homeostasis, the essential biochemical rebalancing of the body, achieved?

The answer is **social integration**. Healthy human cultures have many socially organised homeostatic processes. The primary process is the group paying attention and noticing how everybody is feeling. Social support provided by a well functioning social group plays the major role in restoring well-being.

Social integration works to lift depression in three main ways: sympathy, acceptance and sharing assistance.

First, the person's sympathy group provides sympathy. We are designed to feel sympathy for the loser in a fight, for the person who has just lost something valuable – a relationship, a job, or someone they love.

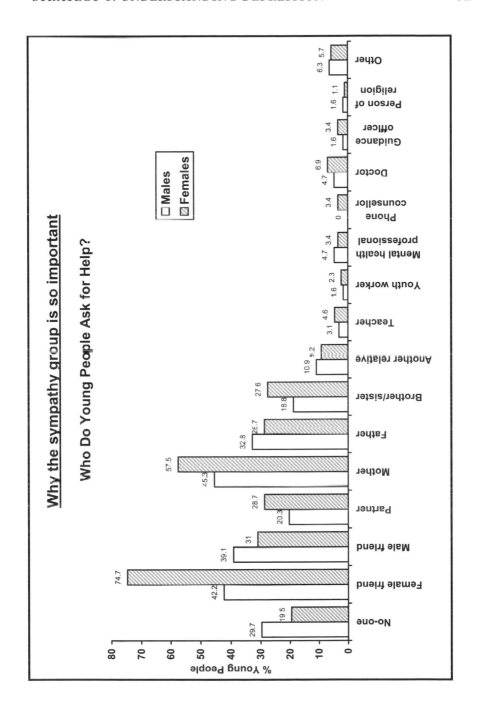

Why the sympathy group is so important

Who Do Young People Ask for Help?

Sympathy means "feeling with". Sympathy works by creating human channels for the negative feelings to flow to earth through the sympathetic listeners. The sympathy group gives comfort, acceptance, understanding and reassurance. We read the loser's body language and when we recognize their emotions and their cause, our brain can generate the same feelings in us.

Second, social integration restores status by simple inclusion and affectionate acceptance, and by enabling the loser to participate in the ongoing cooperative activities of work and play which contribute to the well-being of the group. Cooperative activity gives equal status to everybody. As the individual's social identity moves from loser to player and their status rises, their serotonin levels return to normal and their sense of depression ends.

Third, social integration means that the group cooperates and offers its collective assistance, including strategies, tools, strengths and other resources. The group becomes a team fighting the individual's problem together. In the face of this powerful generosity and support, even complete failure and deep unhappiness is so tempered by honour and gratitude that the person can surrender to their fate and float back up, rather than become mired in depression.

Why is social integration the mechanism which lifts depression and restores well-being?

Because we are designed this way – our evolutionary design is as a socially organised primate species. This mechanism allows human groups to maximise their dominance and internal cohesion. An isolated individual human has almost no chance of survival or genetic success. Similarly, a human group which disintegrates every time there is a dominance contest has little chance of survival.

This mechanism of aggression, depression, sympathy and cooperative interaction is very efficient. It builds social motivation, the sense of mutual interdependence, affection and morale in the group.

How well does this mechanism work?

It works extraordinarily well – when we live in those stable social groups of around 148 members, which our brains are designed and adapted for. An anthropological study of 21 different hunter-gatherer societies around the world found that the average number of people in their villages was 148.4. When researchers examined rural villagers in Samoa, they discovered that the people had extraordinarily low levels of stress hormones in their blood. When an anthropologist attempted to study depression in the Kaluli people in New Guinea, he couldn't find any people who were depressed.

The human mind was designed for getting genes into the next generation. Because social cooperation increases the chances of this genetic success, natural selection has built into our brains an infrastructure for friendship and fairness, including affection, sympathy, gratitude and trust. As parents, you will want to give your children every opportunity to use these inbuilt aptitudes to connect strongly with family, friends and community.

So why is there now this explosive epidemic of depression?

We are suffering this epidemic because we are living outside our biological design envelope, and we have not developed an effective cultural adaptation. It affects so many children now because however hard a child tries, the family, school and the State feel compelled to push them to try harder; however small their social and emotional needs are, there is social pressure for them to make do with less. Consumer culture demands sacrifices of emotional peace, of regular, easy friendships and unhurried fun in order to maximise the productivity which pays for ever-increasing habits of expensive consuming.

To sum up, depression is the opportunity cost of progress – and progress is driven by socially organized dominance striving. We are no longer automatically connected to a stable social group of the right size. Our social groups are now smaller than they have ever been. Worse, they are continually disintegrating before any strong sense of trust, mutual knowledge and affection, or habits of cooperation can be established.

Our cultural norms are eroded and undermined by fashions and pressures far beyond our control. From an economic point of view, we have never been so wealthy or successful. Inside our children's brains in particular, from an emotional and biochemical point of view, it feels like civil war.

Without a stable social group, we automatically feel stress. Without a stable social group it is very difficult to develop and maintain a sympathy group, and almost impossible to be noticed, nourished, and included in cooperative activities. Furthermore, just as in chemistry, when we are not located inside a stable structure of social bonds, the violent collisions of dominance contests increase rapidly.

So stress increases, aggression and depression increase, and the mechanism for restoring balance to our biochemistry – our social supports and social integration – is broken and beyond our ability to repair. We are not biologically designed to continually create our own performance status, we are designed to belong. And children must be given this belong-ing, this secure place, in a social group.

So just ask yourself, if your child felt depressed after some loss or defeat or period of stress, how many people would notice and give them sympathy within two weeks – and include them in some appropriate cooperative activity which would restore their sense of status and well-being? For too many human children, they would have got much better attention if they were a little baboon.

So what is human well-being and how do we maintain it?

Understanding the five elements of human well-being

I remember riding an old bicycle into a fishing village on a tiny island. Children came out to meet me, first a handful, skipping and laughing, confident and curious. We greeted each other with smiles and gestures and unintelligible words. We laughed a lot, and formed a little procession. More and more children came, as they heard the noise. It was an adventure. I didn't know where we were going, but they knew where they were taking me. We passed their tiny houses made of coral and palm fronds with gardens of flowers, banana palms and vegetables. Another child or two would dash out from each house, eager to join in the fun. The children sparkled with well-being, like sunlight on waves on a bright morning. They delivered me safely into the house of the headman, and then flitted away like a flock of brightly coloured wrens.

More than anything, we want our children to shimmer with well-being, to take delight in being alive. We want to them to grow strong, wise, joyful and loving, passionate and confident. Well-being is not wealth and possessions. It is not obedience and achievement. It is a quality of the spirit. We want our children to naturally be in high spirits – not be in low spirits. There is an aboriginal term to describe well-being, *Yorro Yorro*. It means, everything standing up alive in spirit. Well-being is the organising principle of every culture, every social group and each family.

So how do we create well-being?

We foster well-being in two ways. First, we provide food – nutrients for the spirit, not the body. In every culture there are the same four foods; joy, love and connection, wisdom, and empowerment. Just like food for the body, children's spirits need to be fed and nourished every day. They need a flow of joy and a flow of love. They need little, bite-size pieces of wisdom, so that they can digest their daily experiences and grow from them. And they need to be encouraged and assisted to find their own inner power, to follow their own ideas and hunches, the freedom to create, take risks, learn to trust themselves and involve others in making good things together. You as a parent have lots of power to nourish your children with these four foods.

Are these four foods really so vital?

Definitely. Research into the categories of suicide indicates that chronic inability to experience joy leads to depressive suicide. Loss of love and connection leads to egoistic suicide. Inability to find wisdom, consistent social values and meaning, leads to anomic suicide. And persistent powerlessness leads to fatalistic suicide. So these four foods are vital to well-being.

Joy is the most important emotion. It is our inner emotional compass. Not only does it guide us, it guides our social communication and forms the biochemical glue which cements friendships, families and other social groups. It is the basis of reading body language and the basis of our response. The way we give sympathy is guided towards restoring joy in some form. The way we create fairness is by seeking to balance the joyfulness expressed in the body language of each member of the group.

Joy as happiness changes how we think. It helps us recover from stress quicker. It is at the core of our mechanisms for acting – achieving goals, meeting needs, making the best decision. From birth our survival is ensured by the bonding which is created between baby and mother and baby and father, siblings and other caring adults. We are designed to feel pain at a baby's cry and to feel joy at their joy. The brain opiates, endorphin and enkephalin, are released when the baby sees its mother.

Love and connection are more important to humans than to any other species, because we are the most socially interdependent animal. Not only do we need to have a fabric of social connections, but our well-being is dependent on those connections being generally compassionate and sympathetic. Studies of children raised in orphanages have shown the striking damage and developmental retardation which loveless connection produces. We create most of our joy in the company of our friends and family and we nurture and maintain our well-being in small loving groups and networks. Social isolation has a more damaging impact on life expectancy and health than smoking.

Wisdom, seen simply, is all the knowledge and skills which humans make up and share to best maintain well-being. It is not rare and refined – it is much more like porridge – basic daily food. Almost every connection we have includes seeking to catch or share new and helpful wisdom. What we call reason is a subset of our wisdom-making. Our neocortex feels, generalizes, abstracts, runs hypothetical action plans, creates thoughts and realizations, initiates conversations, checks other memories and perceptions.

Human well-being is completely dependent on this daily making and sharing of wisdom.

Children need to learn how to join in this oldest human activity. The quality of the wisdom of each culture and each group is the foundation which generates the sense of identity, meaning and morale for children, and controls how life feels – particularly for children.

This is because wisdom shapes the rules of how everything is shared, what is fair or not fair, allowed or punished, and wisdom informs all the skills of joy, harmony, love, sympathy and adventure which the group uses. Wisdom is structural, built in all these habits and values and actions, and it in turn builds what I would love to call the sociobiochemical bonds that give social groups their cohesion, commitment and endurance.

Empowerment is a vital food for children because children are so easily oppressed, subdued, discouraged. Depression is, as Martin Seligman described it, learned helplessness. Most depressed children have spent years almost pathetically obedient compliant – passive but uninspired and unencouraged to really trust their own intuition, passion and judgement. Many parents, understandably, enjoy placid children. Many schools and teachers and towns prefer emotionally flat children. "Sweet reason", "pacific emotions", "sensible", "level headed" – there are many terms of endearment for children who do not explore or express their power.

Recent research shows that the single greatest drop in creativity in children happens the first year they go to school. Over the last 15 years the prescribing of mood-suppressing drugs for children has increased by nearly 15 times! Childhood is the most important time for all primates, indeed all mammals, to explore, extend and experience their full power. It is vital for

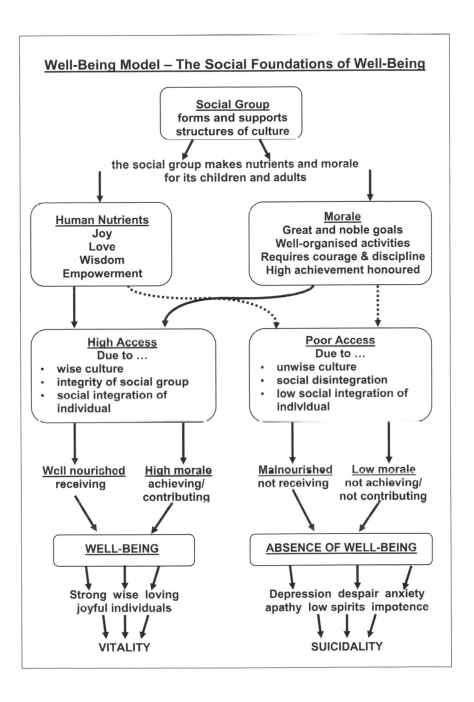

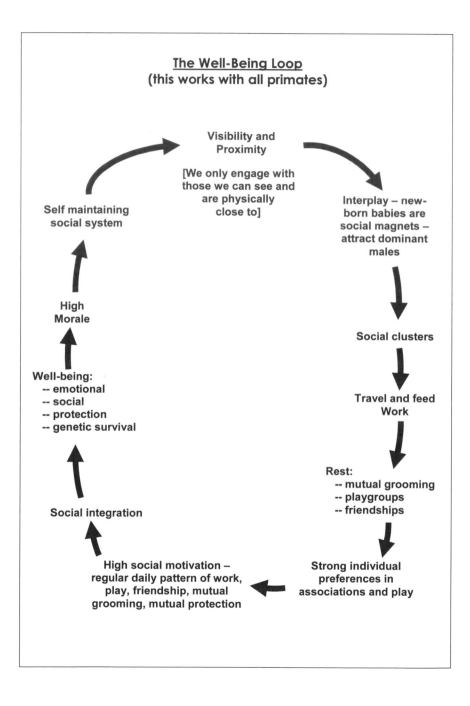

The Well-Being Loop
(this works with all primates)

Visibility and Proximity

[We only engage with those we can see and are physically close to]

Interplay – new-born babies are social magnets – attract dominant males

Social clusters

Travel and feed Work

Rest:
-- mutual grooming
-- playgroups
-- friendships

Strong individual preferences in associations and play

High social motivation – regular daily pattern of work, play, friendship, mutual grooming, mutual protection

Social integration

Well-being:
-- emotional
-- social
-- protection
-- genetic survival

High Morale

Self maintaining social system

cognitive development, physical development, social development, and for social bonds to form.

The second way we foster well-being is by building morale. **Morale** is a completely separate thing from the four foods. Our sense of morale comes from the organised social cohesion and power of the group focused on some very important objective. We must have an active role to play, which is also vital, and we must have a sense of trust in the group and its leaders. Morale always involves training, discipline, commitment and great cooperative efforts. The morale of a group has always been central to its survival and success. When a person becomes demoralised they become very vulnerable to depression, despair and thoughts of suicide.

A group which is in chaos or which has lost its moral regulation produces a high rate of anomic suicides. As children get older, they may develop a hunger for more profound wisdom to inspire their sense of purpose and morale.

So there are five elements that create well-being; **the four foods of joy, love, wisdom and empowerment,** and **morale.**

Remember that they each rely on the day-to-day interplay and supports provided by the social integration of your own community and circle of family and friends. They don't cost money and they can't be bought. Those village children lived on sago, fish, bananas and a few vegetables, in a subsistence economy. If you can give your own children that sense of well-being, you will be rich.

Now let's look at some practical ways to increase your child's well-being and protect them from depression. We will start by looking at ways to increase the flow of nutrients, beginning with joy.

Increasing the flow of joy

Everyday happiness means getting up in the morning, and you can't wait to finish your breakfast. You can't wait to do your exercises. You can't wait to put on your clothes. You can't wait to get out and you can't wait to come home, because the soup is hot.

George Burns

Do not look for rest in any pleasure, because you were not created for pleasure: you were created for Joy. And if you do not know the difference between pleasure and joy you have not yet begun to live.

Thomas Merton

I can but think that the world would be better and brighter if our teachers would dwell on the duty of happiness as well as the happiness of duty; for we ought to be as bright and genial as we can, if only because to be cheerful ourselves is a most effectual contribution to the happiness of others.

Sir John Lubbock

*I finally figured out the only reason to be alive
is to enjoy it.*

Rita Mae Brown

Happiness grows at our own firesides.

Douglas Jerrold

*It is not how much we have, but how much we enjoy,
that makes happiness.*

Charles Spurgeon

He who laughs, lasts.

Mary Poole

Joy is our most important emotion. We do not fall in love without joy; and we cannot maintain love without joy. We only form friendships because in some way we have experienced joy together, and have felt that the other person has enjoyed us and we have enjoyed them. Joy is like the needle of our emotional compass. Whatever difficult, sad or painful emotion we may be having, we can tell which way we want to steer – backwards to joyfulness.

The tragic power of clinical depression is that we lose our compass, and under the influence of despair and depression, our mind generates thoughts that are distorted by pessimism and hopelessness. Joy is very important for parents, because it is the main indicator of your child's well-being.

Shared joy is the primary social glue that binds social groups together. It works before the more powerful social glue of love, and it will form bonds between people who do not feel love for each other. If you go dancing, it is the sharing of the joy of the music and the dancing that creates the magic feeling of oneness. If your child is in the drama group, it is the shared joy of making a play come to life together that binds the group. In religious services, the shared joy of worshipping the same God together, with songs and prayers or other form of ritual, binds the group together and brings out the spirit of community. If your child plays hockey, or netball or golf, it is this same experience of shared joy in playing the game together that is the primary social glue.

If you think about all the organisations that make up your community, almost all of them are voluntary associations where people come together to share their enjoyment of their particular interest or passion. Sharing joy is one of the main threads that weaves the fabric of our community. So as parents, it is important that you increase the flow of joy, and build the habits and skills of making joy in your family, your children and your community.

Joy is our most important emotion, and joy making the most important skill, because joy is like yeast in making bread. Bread made without yeast is very difficult to eat. When you and your children learn to add joy to every possible activity, it makes hard work fun, and effort and unavoidable difficulties lighter and easier to bear.

When we can laugh when the tent falls down and it is raining, it releases our tension and frees us up emotionally and physically, so that we stumble out of the wet wreckage in good spirits to put it up again. When we can laugh at our own stupidity when we are in such a hurry to get to the hockey field that we forget the map, then we forgive each other and avoid the bitterness of blame and resentment. Research shows that most people leave their jobs, not because they can't do them, but because they can't get along with the people. When you teach your children the habits of joy, you give them social skills which will serve them well all their lives.

To increase the flow of joy in your family and for your children, simply ask yourself before you start daily tasks, how can I put more joy into this? How can I make this fun? Joy is easy. Children are designed for joyful play. They enjoy work which feels like fun.

When I was a child, I had the great luck to have an uncle, Uncle Bruce, who was brilliant at making the hardest work feel like the best fun. He gave me the power to choose important adult challenges and let me do it. He was full of enthusiasm and assumed I could do almost anything. He trusted me and took delight in me and what I did. He developed a large sheep property, and I loved to go down with Uncle Bruce and his son, my best friend Davey, on the weekend, to join in. We dug hundreds of holes, put in the fence posts, strung the wire and hung the gates. We dug stones out of the paddocks, looked after the sheep, and shot rabbits. We started work at daylight and usually finished, exhausted, after dark. It was the best way to spend the weekend, and I always looked forward to the next weekend. He just knew how to make hot, dusty hard work into a good and important game together.

One way to broaden the flow of joy is to help other people enjoy your children. You can create many opportunities and occasions for the other adults you know to include your children in doing good things together. The more people who know and enjoy your children, the stronger their social integration becomes. People who have shared joyful experiences together often keep their feelings of affection for years, even decades. A camping trip, picnics, days at the beach swimming and playing Frisbee, community working days at another family's house – there are dozens and dozens of simple activities you and your children can think up and make happen. Joy is easy – but it is easily overlooked.

There is another kind of joy which you can help your children feed on. This is the simple joy of being alive to the beauty all around. You can share the joy of the sky at dawn, the beauty of clouds, the colours of sunset, the new moon, the full moon coming up huge and golden over rooftops or through trees, or clean and wet out of the ocean. You can share the joy of new gold flowers unfurling on a silky oak, the delicious smell coming out of the oven before dinner, the joy of giving someone else something special and watching their face light up when they find out what it is. Helping your children to take joy directly from everyday life helps them in two very valuable ways.

First, they learn to feel grateful for the richness all around them and they learn what a gift beauty is, and how to feel joy just being alive.

Second, this sensitivity to the beauty and the ability to stop and breathe it in is a threshold to transcendent experience, the sense of the sacred and the experience of union. This is not taught in school, but you can gently help your child to cross this threshold and develop their awareness of this profoundness which is in each of us, and which no one can take away.

Only joy balances the hard parts of your children's life. School is not joyful, inherently. It is controlled and rational and often stressful. But it is necessary and relentless. And for most students, school gets harder each year and requires more effort and more time.

So how can you increase the frequency and power of your children's joyful experiences as they get older, to balance and counteract this increasing burden of their education? Many teenage suicides are not caused by trauma or abuse, but because their lives have become a joyless desert. Often their parents are completely devastated, because they loved and cared for these children so much. But love is a different food from joy. Joy by its very nature lifts our spirits. Love alone is often unwittingly oppressive. A lot of teenage drug use and heavy drinking is an attempt to escape this sense of oppression and feel again free, powerful and ecstatic.

If your child likes to surf, let them get you out of bed at dawn two mornings a week, pick up a friend or two and take them for a surf before school. It will change their whole week, increase their status, improve their surfing and make school feel less of a burden. Whatever physical activities your children really love, take the time during the week to give them a couple of sessions.

The other hard parts of your children's life are their losses, griefs, fears and disappointments, and their failures and defeats. Many of these are unavoidable. Pets and loved ones die, friends move away, some of their peers will be cruel, or better than them, hopes and expectations are quite often dashed. You will give them sympathy and understanding, and often help them learn from these hard things to gain an insight or some wisdom. They will not be healed however, until their joyfulness has been restored. It is important that you are able to help them quickly recover their flow of joy, because it is easy for a child to experience a series of losses and defeats. If these feel like an unbroken sequence of misery, they will become demoralised, and their confidence in everything, even their sense of meaning can collapse.

If you have helped them develop strong habits of making joy, and if you have helped develop strong social supports with people who enjoy them and know how to include them in a variety of enjoyable activities, then their resilience and well-being is best protected.

One of the qualities of joy is its spontaneity. If you can open yourself to your children's impulses to create joy, then you can incorporate them into the day. Don't make the mistake of making joy a reward. Then they will learn that whenever they believe they have failed, they should punish themselves by denying themselves joy. This unconscious belief entrenches depression.

Remember that childhood is the time when most people have least status, suffer most defeats, and feel most stupid, awkward and self doubting. So childhood, particularly for the ten years from the age of seven or eight, is a time when the serotonin levels are frequently depressed. So the stronger the flow of joy which you can create with them, the better.

If your child comes home from school itching to go down the river with some friends, it's easy to grab a lettuce, a tomato and a cheap pack of sausages, and have a play and a quick picnic at sunset. You want them to learn how easy it is to have fun in your family. In too many families, getting a bit of spontaneous joy is like trying to squeeze the last toothpaste out of a six-week old tube.

The more you can learn to take joy in their joy, the more you will empower them to create joy for themselves and others in their daily lives.

Joy is in many ways an impediment to our culture. We are a fiercely rational, economically focused culture, with overflowing in-trays, e-mails coming out our ears, and urgent deadlines for every next day. And we have the nerve to treat our children for hyperactivity – where is the mirror? We are trained to put aside both our love of joy and our joy of love. For a working parent, this is a double whammy. Overloaded at work, and overburdened at home. There are never enough hours in the day for either role. We stress just thinking about it.

Joy stands in stark contrast to what is important, the urgent lists of things that have to be done – and the urgent lists are always written on a kind of emotional Velcro. We don't see joy as urgent, do we? But it is.

This is a difficult problem. Why don't we see joy as urgent? There are two reasons. The first is because of the difference between morale and nutrients in creating well-being. Let me explain. When we have a strong sense of purpose – a great and noble object – and a vital, active role to play, then we feel highly motivated and we do not need much emotional food.

Being a parent gives us a very strong sense of purpose, and having a job also gives us a strong sense of purpose, particularly because it helps us support the family. However, our children do not have this same strong sense of purpose – they're not the parents. So their well-being is not maintained primarily by high morale, as ours is. Their well-being, and their development, requires these daily nutrients. This is a big difference between parents and children, but it's not immediately obvious.

The second reason why we don't see joy as urgent is to do with fear and resentment. Parents are the givers – children are the takers. They're as insatiable as baby magpies, more noisy

– and they want to be fed GameBoys and designer jeans. At least magpies are satisfied with grubs. It is very hard not to be resentful, as a parent, and the easiest way to let this resentment out is to withhold joy – believing it is not important.

So what do we fear about joy?

Often we fear the energy. We don't know what to do when our children are out of control in full-on play with other children. We are so trained to restrain ourselves, that often we find it impossible to let our hair down, let our own profound power come out to play, so we can't meet them in their power, and we feel very uncomfortable when they want to explore these intense human capacities they have inherited.

Schools and families both establish powerful norms and rules to suppress this innate human power, and some adolescent depression has been directly linked to children unconsciously depressing this fierce biological power inside themselves. Don't forget that we are a predacious primate species, designed for daily physical play and activity. In adolescence this ferocious human power develops very rapidly and seeks expression – and more than that, it needs to be welcomed, shaped and used by the social group.

Traditional cultures provided rituals and training for this aggressive power because they needed it to survive. Modern rationalist cultures have very little need for this energy, and don't deal with it at all well. In some communities, a large percentage of the 18 to 29 year old males are in jail. Think about how to really welcome and create outlets for this power in your children. When your children can express this power in an atmosphere of enthusiastic acceptance, they feel joy.

Joy can't be rushed. It helps to remember John Lennon's

excellent advice, Turn off your mind, relax and float down-stream. In the surrender to joy, you can learn that you are not your mind. We are schooled to continuously make efforts – to put our best efforts into everything. Realising who you are takes no effort. You will not die when you turn off your mind. The mind is like the surface of the ocean of conscious-ness. Its waves of thoughts and feelings come and go, but when you sink below the surface into the depth of this ocean of consciousness that you are, you realise and experience the peace which passes understanding. You discover the vast, liv-ing emptiness that you are.

You are not your concepts. You are not the waves of feelings and thoughts that sweep your surface. You are not your con-structions of identity, not those fragile assemblies of image and achievement that we cobbled together anxiously. Your real self is a vastness – the Kingdom within. It is a gift that you do not have to earn or fight for. It cannot be taken away from you. In the act of surrender which often accompanies our experiences of deep joy and deep love, we can fall into this inner vastness.

Even small children – in fact, particularly small children – know about this vastness, and they love to fall into it with you or their friends in the magic of play, drunk on the potent spirit of joy.

We need to make a distinction between skilled and unskilled techniques for altering our inner emotional states. In all mam-mal brains, thinking and feeling are interconnected. Humans naturally seek the means to give ourselves positive feelings of joy, excitement and the sense of flow. So our culture has developed lots of tools and technologies to enable us to experi-ence a flow of powerful and changing inner emotions. These include alcohol, drugs, food, television, video and electronic games etc, shopping, possessing and consuming the endless arrays of emotionally charged consumer products. They also include listening to music, watching sports, risk-taking, fighting and breaking the law for the thrill value. Studies have clearly demonstrated that habitually watching television and videos increases aggressiveness by some 40 percent.

WAYS WE ALTER OUR MOODS AND EMOTIONAL STATES	
No skills needed	**Skills are needed**
Alcohol	Friendship
Drugs	Playing with others
Food	Sport
TV	Dancing
Video	Creating
DVD	Adventure
Listening to music	Helping others
Driving	Making music
Shopping	Achieving something
Taking risks	important
	Developing an interest
	Relationships

These technologies are very powerful, and addictive, but they radically weaken our social integration and develop competitive behaviour at the same time as they make cooperative behaviour harder. So they play a powerful negative role in weakening your children's well-being.

But children are biologically designed for touching and physical play. Researchers have found that intellectual development, the development of social and emotional intelligence, the sense of security and well-being all require that children

Benefits of Play

➢ Playing is the only way children develop the skills of creating joy together

➢ Play is how children form most of their friendships and how they sustain and develop these friendships

➢ Play develops imagination and creativity.

➢ Play and talking about what happened is how children develop emotional intelligence.

➢ Play, including sharing and creating good times together, is how children build social capital with each other, as well as trust and a history of satisfying cooperation.

➢ Play builds resilience, resourcefulness, physical coordination, strength, courage, perseverance, versatility, confidence, prowess.

➢ Play develops the brain connections between the frontal and prefrontal lobes and the limbic system, which strengthens the brain's ability to deal with stress – individual homeostasis.

➢ Play helps children meet and build their sympathy group – social homeostasis.

be touched and cuddled and played with from the time they are born.

At the biochemical level, there are indications that this frequent touching makes the brain develop extra receptors which disable the cortisol, the stress hormone.

Children are not born for television – they are born hungry and receptive to joyful play. We parents bring in television, and use it like a cross between a dummy and a babysitter. Joy is food and television is junk food. So to increase the flow of joy for your children help them enjoy active and playful joy together with other children.

Let them choose activities that they want to do and let them feel that they are in charge of making them happen – just making sure that you provide enough help so that they can make them happen.

This is a bit of an art, and every bit of practice you can get will improve your skills, as well as theirs. It is surprisingly easy to establish strong rules about television, if at the same time you are able to be generous in helping them create an increased flow of physically active and cooperative joy.

Rather than limit the time for this physically active play – do the exact opposite. Encourage them to play till they are exhausted and temporarily satisfied. You will build their physical stamina and the strength in their social bonds. They will learn to push themselves, and stretch themselves beyond what they thought they could do and in this energetic childhood play with others, you will be helping to lay the foundations for their morale. These habits of free and active childhood joy help children grow into dynamic and highly motivated adults. There are many examples of this.

John Bertrand was the Australian sailor who broke the dominance of the Americans by winning the Americas Cup after 132 years of unsuccessful attempts. This was an extraordinary achievement by an extraordinarily skilled and determined man. **How did he get to be like this?**

John grew up beside the bay in Melbourne. John's parents and grandparents gave him a childhood rich with joy and freedom – as long as he did his chores and his home work, naturally. John's grandfather, a fisherman, took John and his brother out in his boat very often, from the time he was little. He was encouraged and assisted to muck about in boats as much as he wanted, after school and on the weekends. His parents helped them when he and his brother wanted to take up sailing and then later, to compete.

John followed his passion right through his childhood and it shaped his character and developed his power and determination. This passion and determination fascinated and delighted a whole country in the great sea battles off Fremantle in the summer of 1983. His victory changed the way Australians saw themselves. It strengthened national morale. Throughout history the morale of human groups has always been strengthened by the triumphant victory of their champions. David's victory over Goliath is better known now than 3000 years ago when it happened.

Children are particularly encouraged and inspired by the struggles and triumphs of sporting heroes. David Beckham, Cathy Freeman, Shane Gould, Roger Federer, and Leyton Hewitt each inspire thousands of children to let the joy of their passion drive them to excellence. You want your children to create their own joy directly – not just passively through the television screen.

Increasing the flow of love and connectedness

STRATEGY
4

Remember that the happiest people are not those getting more, but those giving more.

H. Jackson Brown

It is not the level of prosperity that makes for happiness but the kinship of heart to heart and the way we look at the world. Both attitudes are within our power, so that a man is happy so long as he chooses to be happy, and no one can stop him.

Aleksandr Solzhenitsyn

I cannot even imagine where I would be today were it not for that handful of friends who have given me a heart full of joy. Let's face it, friends make life a lot more fun.

Charles R. Swindoll

Whether physical, emotional, psychic, or intellectual, love forms a bridge between the sharers which can be the basis for understanding much of what is not shared between them, and lessens the threat of their difference.

Audre Lord

*If you want happiness for an hour, take a nap.
If you want happiness for a day, go fishing.
If you want happiness for a year, inherit a fortune.
If you want happiness for a lifetime, help somebody.*

Chinese Proverb

Joy increases as you give it, and diminishes as you try and keep it for yourself. In giving it, you will accumulate a deposit of joy greater than you ever believed possible.

Norman Vincent Peale

Your primary goal is to increase your children's well-being by increasing their social integration. This has two parts. The first is to increase the size and active integration of your primary social group – your circle of friends, family, and community. The second part is to increase the integration of your children into this group, which of course includes their friends and friends' families and parents. **The three tools to do this are love, joy, and continuous creativity. Love is your most important tool** – without your love you will not be able to hold all these people together in your heart, and without love growing between them there will be nothing that holds these people together.

Love is the fundamental social glue. Sexual and romantic love form the bonds that bring families into existence. Then the powerful love that we feel for our children forms the bonds that maintain families, and often it is this love that forces us to seek wisdom and learn how to nurture our children's well-being.

What makes us endure all the humiliations and sacrifices of parenting, the stinks and barrows of outrageous nappies? We have been shaped by evolution to love and care about our kin and often this love and sense of interconnectedness comes to the surface and blossoms whenever a member of our extended family becomes ill or dies.

So let your children join in these times of pain and grief, and feel the profound healing of grief that comes when we share our sadness and our love.

When humans evolved, almost all members of the primary social group were related by blood, and mutual love and care enhanced the genetic success of each individual. Now, families are very dispersed, and your primary social group includes lots of people who are not related. But love is still the primary social glue. It is the habits of doing good things together – both work and play – that build the sense of mutual affection and respect. But love takes more. It takes great lovers.

Just think back to your childhood, for a minute. Who were the great lovers? Who were the people who had the biggest hearts, who best loved you and the rest of the family, or the rest of the neighborhood? Were you lucky? Did you have one or two of these extraordinarily loving people in your childhood? When the family or the neighborhood has a few of these people in it, something quite magic happens. Somehow, the greatness of their love melts people together, bringing out a sense of belonging that is deep and satisfying – and somehow liberating, so that you feel freer to be yourself, far more certain of your worth than you could ever feel without this powerful blessing. Just a few of these people can release the spirit of community – as hard to see but just as gently real as the perfume of jasmine on warm night air. What would it be like, if you chose to become one of these profound lovers, in your family, in your community? What gifts you would be able to give your children – and yourself! How would you do it?

There are **three secrets** that these people have learnt. If you can learn them, you can teach them to your children.

Secret one – your huge heart

The **first secret** is about how huge your heart is really. Many people think their heart is quite small and fragile. They think that when they love two or three people – or maybe six – that their heart is full. The secret is that your heart is infinite. You can hold 100 people in your heart, you can hold every child in the world in your heart, you can hold every baby whale, every puppy, everyone who ever suffered loss and grief and misery. You can hold the whole world in your heart. How did Nelson Mandela create a healing and a new beginning for millions of South Africans? First, he held them in his heart, in love, in an ordinary, human heart, just like yours, no different.

YOUR HUGE HEART

Who do you hold in your heart?

Write in all the names or draw pictures.

Exercise: photocopy for each family member to do together.

Secret two – the certainty of love

The **second secret** is about learning the certainty of Love. I was taught this secret by an old black man, a grey haired preacher who had given his life to work for civil rights for his people, and to make them strong and united by their love for one another. When he was a young man his brother had died in his arms, shot in the chest by a sheriff for sitting in the wrong seat in a movie theatre in Mississippi. Brother John Perkins had every reason to be bitter and hateful. He had been imprisoned, and beaten nearly to death. Somehow, like Nelson Mandela and Mahatma Gandhi, he had learnt about the certainty of Love.

Usually, we are uncertain about love. If we love someone, we continuously read their body language and analyse their every action – to see if they still really love us. Whenever we get a hint that their love for us is uncertain, we back off, hurt and angry. Now at the same time, of course, they're doing the same thing – they read our body language – and when they see us back off, they back off. So we play this painful game of ping-pong, on and on, each reinforcing our beliefs in the uncertainty of Love. Have you ever played this game? It is continuously stressful, it takes a lot of emotional energy, keeps us anxious and can leave us bitter and confused – and often cynical.

Love is an act of choice, and when you choose to be certain in your love for someone, suddenly, and wonderfully, you are free.

It doesn't matter anymore whether the other person is certain in their love for you. If you hold someone in your heart – how can they get out? They can't. But now a funny thing happens. Once you are certain in your love for that person, it is very

MAP YOUR LOVING CONNECTIONS

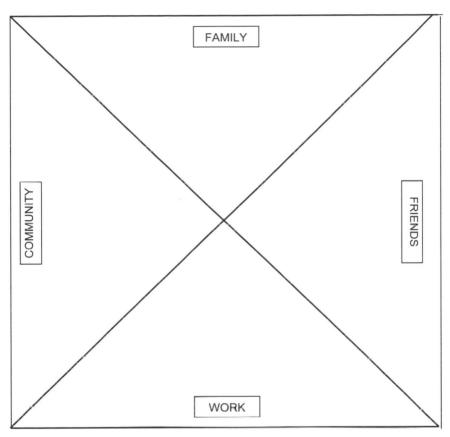

The centre of the diagram is your heart
Put the people in your life on the map at the distance from your
heart that you feel them to be. Put a dot for each person and
write their name or initial alongside the dot. (10 minutes)
Then colour code your map, using a coloured circle around each
dot. (5 minutes)

*Kin are all the people you are related to. Kith are all the people
you feel something for – more than just acquaintances

COLOUR CODE
1. Love   Yellow
2. Growing relationship   Green
3. Conflict   Red
4. Wisdom   Blue
5. Joy/adventures/
   feel good   Orange

Exercise: photocopy for each member of your family to do together

relaxing. It takes much less energy, and you are quite free to just love them, and to notice whatever they are feeling, and relate to them in that space with love. Usually, quite unconsciously, they read your body language and feel the certainty of your love.

This makes an enormous difference to how they feel. They trust you now and let you in, because they know they are in your heart. They feel free to open themselves up to you – and in this flowering, which blossoms as your love nurtures them, you see their beauty.

What a gift! You feel so blessed by this gift that often you know you have been given much more than you have given them – and yet they cherish their gift from you, the certainty of your love for them.

Try this out for yourself. Try it with little children first, because they are so easy to love and respond with such joy. Almost from birth, children learn to read body language, and if they sense that you love them, and that you take delight in them, they will play with you and you will start to learn how to be certain in your love.

Then try it with people that you meet. Try it with awkward adolescents. Practice it with your children and with their friends. Like any new skill, at first you have to be quite conscious and clear in your intent. When you get the hang of it, it will become easy. Just don't force yourself – you don't have to be a Jesus.

Secret three – our well-being is connected

The **third secret** is that well-being is connected. When your children are doing well, you are doing well. When your community is strong and happy, you have well-being and happiness. When you love people in this way, you are not in competition with them any more. You can enjoy their joy, and feel for them and give them support when they are miserable. You move beyond competitive individualism. Great love sets you free, free in yourself, and free to nurture the fabric of family, friends and community for yourself and your children. Teach your children to care for everyone's wellbeing and they will learn this sense of connection.

Western culture is powered by greatly increasing our habits of competition – and the need to display how good we are through our possessions. Children are particularly vulnerable to these habits. Your children are currently exposed to around 20,000 ads each year – each one carefully crafted to apply maximum emotional pressure. This pressure is negative. The fundamental message underneath every advertisement is that you are **not** okay – until you buy this next product – in fact, you have already fallen behind your peers, the smarter and more successful ones who already own the product. The cumulative message of this avalanche is that your children come to believe that their identity itself and their sense of meaning in their life depends on endlessly buying new products. Consumerism uses great technological power to tap into false magic beliefs that we thought we had left behind.

More and more children really believe that their identity is as fragile as the brands of shoes, clothes and accessories that they wear. You as a parent have to do battle with this potent stupidity.

This is why love is such an important food for children. Only the real experiences of loving connectedness to a known and trusted social group have the power to help children gain a sense of their identity and worth which is resilient enough to withstand these corrosive forces.

So how do you use the three tools of **love, joy and creativity** to build these real experiences of loving connectedness?

The *first* step is to realise that there are these two quite different kinds of connectedness, automatic connection and connection based on performance. Automatic connections come from just being a member of a particular group. Your children are automatically members of your extended family. They are automatically members of the school community. If you belong to a church, they are automatically members of the congregation.

If your neighbourhood has an active sense of community, then your children are automatically members of the community. The more social activities that you and your children participate in, with these different social groups, the stronger this sense of belonging – this automatic connection – becomes.

The more you're able to use your creativity in planning and organising a flow of these social activities, and the more you are able to make these activities friendly, loving and joyful, the more your children develop their sense of well-being. In this way they get to know a wide range of people of all ages, and feel at home with them. Some of these relationships will become friendships.

Automatic connections are very important for children, and you as parents create and nurture these connections. It doesn't take much effort to do this, just a bit of creativity. If the people in your street don't know each other very well, organise a

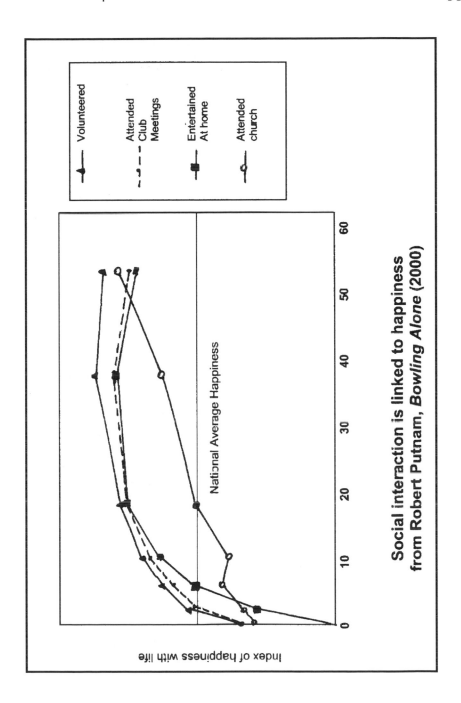

Social interaction is linked to happiness
from Robert Putnam, *Bowling Alone* (2000)

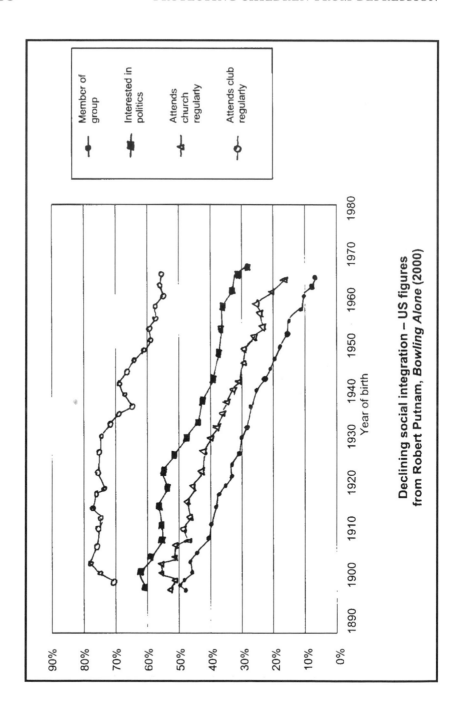

**Declining social integration – US figures
from Robert Putnam, *Bowling Alone* (2000)**

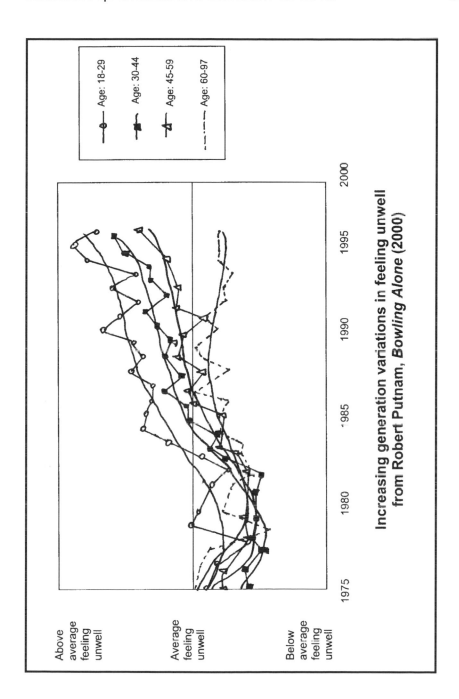

Increasing generation variations in feeling unwell
from Robert Putnam, *Bowling Alone* (2000)

EFFECTS OF SOCIAL ISOLATION

In young children:
- Developmental damage and delay
- Emotional damage
- Low social skills
- Low emotional intelligence
- Chronic stress problems
- Cortisol damage to vermis causing:
    - GABA dysregulation of limbic system
    - Aggressive tendencies
- Cortisol damage to hippocampi causing:
    - Learning difficulties
    - Poor memory

Generally:
- Lowered serotonin production
- Lowered mood
- Pain felt in anterior cingulate gyrus
- Increased anxiety
- Increased vulnerability
- Reduced/no social roles and social capital
- Increased risk of obsessive compulsive disorder
- Reduced wisdom sharing
- Increased stress
- Reduced joy
- Damage to immune system
- Damage to heart arteries
- Increased cholesterol
- Increased risk of heart attack and stroke
- Increased alcohol consumption
- Decreased morale
- Decreased emotional stability
- No social homeostasis
- No love

street party at someone's house, or even in the street. Invite everybody, and ask them all to bring a plate to share. You will be amazed at how much fun everybody can have at a simple, afternoon get-together – and at how much more friendly the street feels to your children after such an event.

Research has shown that burglaries go down in direct proportion to how many of your neighbours you know. I lived in a street where we had street parties a few times a year, including a Christmas party, for 20 years. Sixteen children grew up in the street and it was wonderful to see how much they enjoyed this rich sense of connection and belonging. So too of course did the adults. In 20 years, there was *only one* minor burglary.

The *second* kind of connectedness, connection based on performance, is much more fragile and difficult for children in particular. This relies on skills and successful effort. Membership of lots of groups is like this. You can only be in the choir if you can sing in tune and have a good voice. You can only be in the hockey team, or the netball team, or the soccer team, if you can play well enough. For your children, many of their peer groups which they would like to be part of, are performance based. So often they are disappointed – and socially excluded – because they are not good enough. You have to hunt around to find a group at their level, or get them into a training program and encourage them until they are good enough to make the grade.

But the most important performance-based connections are **friendships** and **intimate relationships. So teach your children how to be good friends. Let them get lots of practice.** Encourage them to bring their friends home and welcome their friends into your family and your social groups. Help them create good games which they enjoy. You have to teach them how to play fair, how to share things and how to take turns. And you have to teach them to understand the boundaries of play – cruelty, teasing, bullying, causing pain, fear or misery are not okay.

But just learning these things alone is not enough. Many children, who have learnt these skills never master the real goal – learning to be a good friend. At heart, they stay competitive individuals, at the mercy of other people's friendship skills and choices. You want your children to learn how to be good friends, and gain the power and freedom and rich social supports which only come with the mastery of friendship.

There are three things which you can teach your children to help them become good friends.

First, teach them to enjoy their friends as people, to notice and take delight in their personalities and ways of being themselves.

Second, teach them to care for their friends, to notice the little signs that show how they are feeling inside and to respond with sympathy and active assistance.

Third, teach them how to make friendship itself conscious.

Talk with your children about friendship, as an important skill that you want them and their friends to learn. In your daily conversations, you can easily explore their stories from the day within the framework of friendships. What did they really notice and enjoy about particular children? How come that particular game was such good fun? Who was miserable today? When you as the parent can show your sympathy alongside their sympathy for other children, this powerfully reinforces their caring nature.

Then you can explore with them what they were able to do, if anything, to show their sympathy and to give their loving support. You want them to know how much you love and value your child for their warm heart and their generosity, even if they were not actually able to do anything useful that time.

But you want your children to grow more skilful and powerful as friends, so, wherever possible, take two more small steps in these conversations.

The *first* step is talking about unfinished friendship business. From the unfinished business of today's experiences, did they learn anything new about their friends and how might they do things differently tomorrow. How can they organise to play that really good game again? If someone spoilt the game today, how can they stop that happening tomorrow? Who will help them do this? If someone was really sad today, what could they do to cheer them up or be their friend tomorrow?

The *second* step is friendship dreams. What do they fancy doing next, and who with?

The more you can join in these dreams and plans for doing good things with friends, the more you build their confidence and creativity as friends. You must do this very gently, mainly as an encouraging listener or sounding board. The power must stay with them – it's easy to take over. **Your aim is for them to feel inspired by their own desire and imagination – not yours.**

As the parent, you are coaching your children in the skills of friendship and loving connection, just the same as if you were coaching them at netball or swimming. They need to feel the value of these skills – initially by simply feeling the deep pleasure and security of being loved, and then more and more, the delight and satisfaction they get from loving others

<u>WHY CHILDREN LOSE A SENSE OF COMMUNITY</u>

COMMUNITY GROUPS GROW APART OVER TIME

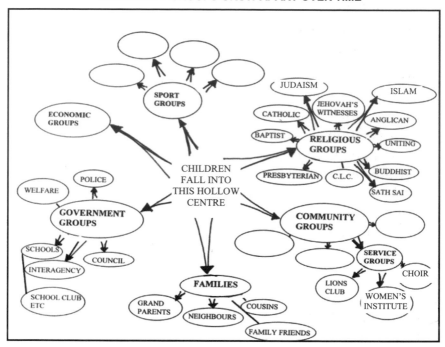

1. Natural differentiation – over time the groups that make up a community grow further apart.

2. Ageing members – almost all community groups have ageing members – and it becomes more and more difficult for children and youth to join in.

3. The rate of change of residents is faster than the rate at which the social fabric is woven, friendships made, etc.

4. These groups are shrinking in size.

well, until they understand that these patterns of giving and getting joy and help weave the strong net of social support and well-being.

You can help them focus on these skills, practice them regularly, and feel the challenge of stretching themselves and the pleasure of success.

Often, children develop their tenderness and compassion by playing with smaller children, including babies, and by having pets. Puppies make the best pets, because they are so affectionate, and they tune in to human body language, so they are very responsive playmates. Female puppies are better than male puppies, because they can have puppies –and almost all children are very moved and excited by seeing these tiny creatures and watching how lovingly the mother cares for them.

Statistically, almost 60% of children will not have a little brother or sister, to help them learn the very delicate skills of nurturing and enjoying babies and little children, but you as the parent can create other ways for them to gain this very important human knowledge.

Also, help your children form friendships with older children and adults, including aunts and uncles, grandparents and older people.

There is always a natural element of competitiveness between peers, but usually this does not arise where there is a big age difference. So the play and interaction is primarily cooperative, and this balances the peer competitiveness which dominates school interaction.

Children are very sensitive to threats to their status, so they often fiercely conceal their real fears and thoughts from their peers, parents and teachers, but feel more able to talk freely to close, older friends who have no power over them. **A common feature of adolescents who become violent or depressed is their secrecy or isolation** – the fact that they did not have anybody who was able to encourage them to honestly share their real feelings.

Children are also very sensitive to stress – your stress – and can easily feel quite unable or unwilling to open up to you because of this. In 1999, a survey of 1000 children found that their most common wish for their parents was that they would be less stressed and tired by work.

Love offers you a great gift. The more you see all of what you do as expressions of love intended to nurture well-being for yourself and the other people in your life, and the more easily you can hold people in your heart, the more you can relax.

As a boy, I had wonderful aunts and uncles, including some ring-ins. Among them, my two Auntie Marys, Uncle Dean, Auntie Phil and Auntie Freda. The most loving five people that I ever knew, were also the most joyful. They knew how to enjoy everybody that they loved, and they were so good at loving that they enjoyed almost everybody who crossed their path. And every day, this love and joy was given back to them. Each of them experienced their full share of death and grief and heartache, and yet this orientation to love didn't just bring them healing, it made their hearts bigger. They were the "great lovers" of my childhood, and they still inspire me. I always knew that I was in their hearts.

The more the people in your life know that you hold them in your heart, the more love they will give you – and this will give you peace and the sense of joyful well-being, which you in turn can give to your children.

Organising the transmission of wisdom

*First a seeker after wisdom, then a finder,
then a hunter after more invisible game*

Rumi

*All seasons are beautiful for the person
who carries happiness within.*

Horace Friess

*To me every hour of the day and night
is an unspeakably perfect miracle.*

Walt Whitman

*Simply seek wisdom. Pay absolutely no attention to your
ego. It will wither away, like the tail on the tadpole.*

Sai Baba

Too many wish to be happy before becoming wise.

Susanne Curchod Necker

I have lived on the lip of insanity, wanting to know
reasons, knocking on a door. It opens.
I've been knocking from the inside!

Rumi

If in our daily life we can smile, if we can be peaceful
and happy, not only we, but everyone will profit from it.
This is the most basic kind of peace work.

Thich Nhat Hanh

Children need wisdom

There is an old Sufi saying that the most important thing that happens in the world every day is the transmission of wisdom.

But wisdom has become invisible. We want tangible results – more money, more profits, a higher standard of living. Overburdened with this pressure to maximise material progress, we have let the concept of wisdom slip below our radar screens. Now we primarily watch for signs of "objective" rational intelligence, and for powerful, useful knowledge. For a long time, it has been out of fashion to go inside and find out who we are.

However, I am convinced that the Sufis are right. Like me, you might also have noticed rational intelligences building logging roads into the Amazon, announcing plans for another 20 million passenger flights each year, building 20 new jails in California – but only one new university.

It is much easier to teach children to act with rational intelligence than to do the difficult work of growing wise. It is precisely the actions of unwise rational intelligence that are causing our oceans to rise and our children to fall into depression.

So what is wisdom – and how do we transmit it?

The word stem "wis" comes from the old English *wit* (or *witan*) which in turn derives from the Sanskrit dhatu *wid* – to know, and from the Latin *videre* – to see. The suffix "-dom" comes from an old English word meaning "decree or judgement". Hence, the word wisdom literally means "judgement seen".

So wisdom is an understanding arising from a capacity to see things as they really are and act accordingly. Lao Tzu taught his students the importance of being centred and grounded and seeing how things happen. When we are centred, we return ourselves to emotional balance. When we are grounded, we feel the natural weight and gravity of our true nature. When we see how things happen, then we can help things happen wisely.

The test of wise seeing is wise action, seeing that results in good, effective judgement, and good outcomes. For Lao Tzu, the wise leader in any group was the person with the widest consciousness, who was centred and grounded, and who acted on behalf of the well-being of the whole. Now and from now on, we and our children face the challenge of acting wisely, consciously seeing how things happen which destroy or nurture the well-being of the whole earth.

So the test of wisdom is that it nurtures the well-being of the whole, in some way. For aboriginal elders, their organising principle was that everything should be standing up alive in spirit, and the circles of elders created vast fields of "seeing" – of wise collective consciousness, out of which came their profound understanding, their tribal Wisdom.

This capacity to see, which is at the heart of wisdom, creates the capacity to understand, and out of this seeing and understanding comes knowledge. The easy bit to teach is the knowledge: it is harder to awaken the capacity to understand – and it is far more difficult to develop the capacity to see. As Anthony Brilliant says, " education has a lot to learn."

If we open up this business of seeing we come to the deepest question – "Who is seeing?"

"Who is the seer?" This is the same question as "Who am I?" All wisdom traditions have created trainings, practices and exercises to lead the seeker towards an answer. What I think I am, and, indeed, how much I think, radically change my ability to see – and what it is that I see as real.

The great religious wisdom transmissions divide and travel on three different pathways to answer this question. The first pathway is to try to copy the behaviour of the God, of the prophet and of the Saints. Christianity and Islam follow this pathway. The second pathway is to use disciplined practice to control the mind; mindfulness. Buddhism and the various forms of yoga follow this pathway.

The third pathway is self-realisation – turning the mind around to see itself – and when this is achieved, you realise in a moment that you are not the feelings and constructions of your mind – that you are living conscious emptiness, in which everything appears and disappears. This is why the quest for wisdom leads within, and why the end of wisdom is freedom. Jesus said the kingdom of heaven is within. The Sufis teach that the heart and mind are infinite, and that those who have great wisdom shine with the inner light.

The transmission of wisdom is at the heart of every culture – but often ossified or lost sight of in the focus on the knowledge and the habits. **Wisdom is how we create the knowledge and skills which give us the power to maintain well-being.** We need the knowledge and skills to feed and shelter ourselves and our families, to protect them from danger and ill health, and to teach them how to thrive and to navigate their way through society.

But human well-being requires more than this, as the figures on violence, depression and suicide clearly show us. It requires emotional well-being – and this requires a strong fabric of social relationships, and a sense of purpose and morale. Human well-being also requires a strong fabric of relationships between people and all the creatures, plants and ecosystems of the earth. No modern culture has even begun to weave this fundamental eco-social fabric – and yet our children's well-being relies on this completely.

The challenge of the transmission of wisdom will always be with us. The more we realise who we really are – this living void – the more clearly we see, and we see how little we really need to live in joy and love. The more we awaken in ourselves and each other the capacity to see and understand, the more wisely and harmoniously we are able to act. At the same time, we need to share our wisest knowledge, realising its limitations.

No doubt you have your own views about wisdom – and these views maybe fierce and certain, or mild and vague. Humanity's longest running battles have all been disagreements about wisdom – whatever side we are on, God is definitely on it too. For this reason, it is worth establishing different fields of wisdom, to minimise possible areas of disagreement, find common ground and help you work out ways to cooperatively work with others to increase the wisdom of all the children.

Nine fields of wisdom

1 **Micro wisdom** – the earliest field in which as babies, we begin to develop our capacity to see and understand; recognising loved ones, sharing smiles, playing eye games, expressing needs and feelings – getting food and attention, seeing how life happens and how we the participate in its creation.

2 **Morality** – the capacity for seeing and understanding fair-ness, kindness and cruelty, helping and sharing, recognising right and wrong

3 **Ecological wisdom – ignored except in tribal cultures** – the capacity for seeing the natural world, developing understanding and knowledge of how to love, nurture and protect all the populations of plants and creatures which form your ecosystems and are your homeland

4 **Social and emotional intelligence** – a capacity for seeing the social and emotional worlds, leading to a range of skills from understanding and expressing emotions to the complex skills involved in maintaining happy extended families, thriving communities, joyful children

5 **Practical wisdom** – seeing how to keep the boat afloat, food on the table, a roof over your heads

6 **Religious wisdom** – serving spiritual beings

7 **Mindfulness** – the capacity to be consciously present in each moment. From this capacity to see, people have developed the skills and disciplines at the heart of yoga, buddhism and several other teachings which bring the mind to a point of stillness and clear flow, taming the inner nature, living consciously in the present moment and, in Thich Nhat Hanh's

memorable phrase, smiling at habit energies – patterns of conditioned thought which interfere with our ability to see.

8 **Self-realisation** – turning the mind around to see itself – and discovering the Ocean of consciousness at the core of your being, realising there is no separateness, just a oneness, the dearest freshness, the unspeakable freedom which is your truth

9 **Eldership** – the field of wisdom entered because of the responsibilities for other people. From this capacity to see comes the capacity to understand how well-being occurs. From this seeing and understanding come all the skills and knowledge which people gather to nurture the well-being of the whole – the whole family, the whole person, the whole community, the whole creation. We are at the point of needing to turn ourselves into global elders, gathering the skills and fabrics of relationships to nurture the whole earth – not just our group, not just our religion, not just our species.

Looking at wisdom from these nine different perspectives, these nine different categories will help you be more precise and creative in the wisdom you search for, both for yourself and for the children in your care.

Wisdom is a capacity of understanding which has created the many skills of joy, of friendship and loving connection, of nurturing well-being and the sharing of power. Transmitting wisdom is about developing both self-awareness, and nurturing this ability to see the well-being and needs of the people and creatures around us. And wisdom always includes a sense of purpose which is based in the desire to serve and maintain this interconnected well-being, in ways which fit our talents and interests, and challenge us. So wisdom includes the skills and knowledge to understand and manage our thoughts and feelings, the ability to create flows of joy and flows of love, compassion and affection, the abilities to find wisdom, to create wisdom and to share it. Wisdom includes the ability to empower people and to build and maintain morale within our social groups. Can you see that this pretty well sums up your challenge as parents?

As parents, we seek the wisdom to maintain our own and our children's well-being. We look for all the ways we can help our children learn wisdom, so that they become able to maintain their own well-being. **We want them to learn enough wisdom to be able to nurture and develop their relationships and their own children and families.** And we are not just parents. We are members of workplaces and organisations and social groups, including our culture, our religion, our state, our nation, our species and our planet. So in varying degrees, we seek wisdom to maintain the well-being of these other groups we belong to. And part of this usually involves working to transmit the wisdom we have found to other people who also need to care about the well-being of each particular group.

Wisdom is an everyday thing. Tich Nhat Hanh talks about the importance of contemplation. When he is facing a problem and cannot see how to resolve it, he gives himself time for contemplation, until he can see into the problem with compassion and understanding. Every time you think about what is the best thing to do here, in a particular situation, you are thinking about what is the wisest thing to do – what will increase or protect our well-being most effectively, and how will I go about it?

Very often, when you think about a situation, you remember wisdom you have already learnt – or you create some wisdom from inside yourself, by seeing consciously and freshly, allowing your understanding to arise.

And often, you ring up a few friends and talk with them, sharing how you each see things, seeking their wisdom until you find that blend of knowledge and skills to best help you now. Almost all conversations that we have include a strand of wisdom transmission – seeking, sharing and creating it.

WHERE DOES YOUR WISDOM COME FROM?

Questions:
1. Who were the greatest elders in your life?
2. What gifts did they give you?
3. What has their wisdom or example helped you to do?
4. Who changed your life?
5. Who gives you your best wisdom now?
6. How do you give wisdom?
7. What are you wrestling with right now?
8. Who have you given some wisdom to lately?

Have this conversation with several people, your partner, children or some friends

---

You can teach your children to think in these terms. Emotional intelligence is the basic building block of wisdom.

So *first*, you can help your children come to know themselves, what makes them feel good or bad, and what their feelings are called. You can help them recognise how their feelings are connected to the way they see things, the way they understand things, and how much power they feel they have to influence what happens.

And *second*, you can help your children come to know their

friends' feelings and habits, the things they are good at, and the things they are bad at. Your aim is to develop your children's awareness and insight, as well as their personal and social skills.

Two key communication skills

There are two simple skills which can help you do this, and you may already be very familiar with them. The first skill is **active listening** – sensitively tuning in to what they are feeling when they are talking, and then respectfully saying back to them what they seem to be feeling, and their reasons for it. Don't argue with them or judge them, don't comfort or distract them. Your aim is just to give them basic understanding. If you do this skillfully, they will feel that you have heard and understood them.

So for example, you might say, "You seem really hurt because Peter didn't ask you to go the beach with him." Or, "You really love that puppy, the way she plays with you." Or, "It sounds like you're getting pretty angry at how this new biology teacher is treating you." This skill will not only help your children become more aware of their feelings, it helps the energy of the emotion discharge – like electricity flowing to earth through a conductor. It also builds the trust between you, and you then have more power to explore their stories more fully, and help them gain an insight or develop a new strategy, or let go of a limiting belief.

The second skill is simply but honestly **sharing** your stories and feelings with them – including some of your fears and failures. This helps your children get to know you as a person, and reassures them that everybody, of all ages, wrestles with life and the getting of wisdom, to achieve happiness and well-being. They will not just learn about your feelings however. They will start to the see how lots of your actions and intentions, and the way you make decisions and judgments, are organised around the principle of serving the well-being of the whole, by seeking the wisest course of action. This is a very valuable thing for your children to learn – many children never learn this, and simply spend their childhoods trying to squeeze more out of their parents – often resenting or blaming them at the same time.

HEART TO HEART TALKING

This is an ancient social custom from one of the tribes who live in the Amazon rainforest. It is something that friends do when they meet in the forest.

1. Find somewhere comfortable and peaceful (on a fine day it's lovely to go into the garden or any beautiful place).

2. Make yourself comfortable with cushions, eiderdown or blankets and lie down, side by side, looking up at the trees (or the ceiling).

3. Take 20 minutes each to just talk, from your heart. The other listens silently.

4. After each of your has spoken, and listened, have a conversation about whatever moves you.

Do this with one of your children, do it with a friend, do it with your partner

Wisdom moves outwards and inwards

From this basis of emotional intelligence, wisdom moves in two directions, inwards and outwards. Wisdom moves inwards into exploring and realising our inner profoundness. Without this, children just think that they are their latest desire or feeling or belief, and are always at the mercy of the next wave of emotion. You can lead your children into the depth of who they are, so that they come to sense their profound nature, and together you can enjoy this profoundness of being, the greatest gift of human evolution.

How to bless children

You can help them come to rest in the cave of their deep hearts, and find this peace at the core of their being. Whenever you see a child deeply, and simply greet them from your own loving awareness, they feel blessed. Practice this skill of letting your consciousness connect deeply with their consciousness, without any agenda. You will feel blessed too.

Wisdom moves outwards into exploring and realising the interconnectedness of well-being. You want your children to learn to notice and understand the links and structures of relationships in families and social groups, for humans and for all living creatures, and you want your children to learn how to nurture and maintain these connections. Well-being and wisdom are both ecological; that is, they rely on a living web of relationships.

Your children need your help – to learn to move their focus of attention in these two directions, inner and outer. Their mind will see completely different things – and come to see things completely differently – as they change their mental focus and awareness.

Your children will also need very gentle assistance to learn to become mentally silent, so that when they sink into themselves their mind doesn't keep interrupting them with messages from everywhere else, and they can free themselves to move inwards. When they shift their minds outwards, to the inner world of a friend, or a family of rosella, then they will only be able to enter these other worlds with their silent awareness. If they keep getting interrupted by their own ego jumping up and down like an impatient three-year-old, then they will not be able to develop their insightfulness.

Make the time to talk with your children every day, in a relaxed and intimate way. You want your children to learn how emotional well-being comes from developing self-awareness and sensitivity to others' wants and feelings as well. Then they can learn the skills and strategies to make good things happen – for themselves, alone and with their friends – and how to anticipate and avoid stress and conflict, and also how to repair hurt feelings and frustrated plans.

Encourage your children to talk openly and deeply with other people also, both with other children and with the adults whom they know and trust. You want them to learn that this business of seeking and making wisdom is a natural social activity. You want them to be very comfortable about accessing the wisdom and resources of their entire social group – because once they have learnt this, they are never isolated, and they can almost always gather enough power and knowledge to meet any challenge.

The key ingredient in a good social support system is not sympathy, important though that is. The key ingredient is sufficient wisdom and power to restore well-being. And as you know, you have to be quite skilful in how you connect with people and how you tap their knowledge. Your children need these skills, as well as a good social support system.

Some men are not good at seeking and transmitting wisdom. Too many men use aggression and dominance to control their families. Women generally are far more involved in seeking and transmitting wisdom to maintain the well-being of children. And yet, most books of wisdom make out that it is a complex and esoteric subject – best left to learned men, priests, scholars, rabbis and mullahs. This is rubbish.

Every culture likes to gather its wisdom into a complex, integrated system of knowledge and rules, carved on tablets of stone and controlled by the men at the top of the dominance hierarchy.

But wisdom changes – it is an adaptive strategy. In the words of the Zen saying, you can't catch running water in a bucket. Every human is biologically designed to sense their own well-being and to seek the best ways to adapt to their changing needs and circumstance.

Children share their wisdom with each other at primary school, and with members of their sympathy group, that small group of individuals whom they specially trust and care about. As adults, we continue to share and hunt for wisdom with each other, also primarily with members of our sympathy group.

Becoming an elder

But most adults start to become elders – sharing responsibility for the well-being of social groups. Our focus on well-being changes from being self-centered to that sense of interconnected well-being. Often, we care for the well-being of several groups. This challenge of becoming a wise and loving elder is the most invigorating and satisfying thing many people do, helping to nurture the well-being of a large and complicated group of people, trying to outwit and defeat greedy or cruel individuals, creating ways to bring people together so that they can learn to love and care about each other's griefs and joys, and the earth they live on.

When you have made this fabric of living interplay, formed out of all the different kinds of interactions and relationships, then the wisdom of the whole group flows between the members to where it is needed, because people know and care about each other. The group comes to notice itself over time, provided it connects regularly enough, and as long as people remain members of the group. Then the group itself develops a collective consciousness.

Emile Durkheim, who was one of the founders of Sociology, also wrote about how groups develop a collective conscience, the shared set of values and norms which the group uses to regulate its own moral behaviour.

Your children are growing up when the rate of social change is so high that their social groups decay and disintegrate faster than they grow. Children only get social support from three places – their family, their sympathy group and their primary social group. This is not only where they get their joy and love, but where they get their wisdom, and where they learn to share it. When the rate of social change is so high, these primary social groups don't just disintegrate, they lose their ability to transmit wisdom. They become confused and demoralised about their values, the adults and elders lose their knowledge and authority to guide and regulate behaviour.

For parents, this problem of wisdom transmission is serious. Who knows your children well enough to have worthwhile insights into their personalities and needs, and to have some loving wisdom for them? How many people have known your children for more than five years?

Your children need to learn how to get wisdom from lots of people, easily and naturally, whenever they need it. Also, your primary social group needs to learn to notice the well-being of your children and to skillfully give them wisdom and assistance whenever they need it.

How do you organise this?

First of course, you have to organise the ongoing flow of social activities so that they can interact and come to know and enjoy each other. Create picnics, meals together, daytime parties and visits, working bees, games nights, sleepovers – anything that people enjoy. Then you can encourage people to take an interest in your children. Ask them about how they think your children are. You can ask them if maybe they would be able to talk to them about how they going, or about a particular issue, maybe give them a little bit of advice, and share some of their own stories.

You have almost unlimited power to initiate and foster a variety of shared activities which build friendly, ongoing relationships between your children and the adults in your social group whom you know and trust.

Don't be afraid to share your stories and concerns about how your children are going. Don't keep them a secret. Often child-rearing becomes a kind of competition between parents and between families – often between related families. This is a bad idea – because it stops the flow of wisdom.

If you hide your difficulties and failures then how can you ask for help? How can you be offered other people's wisdom? How do you get wisdom then?

Just when you need it most your pride can prevent you from simply asking for it. You often need to be able to sit down with a good friend or two, and just take time to tip all the pieces of the puzzle on the table and push them around together until you come up with the wisest way forward.

The organising principle of wisdom is always well-being. We maintain well-being by four different actions; nurturing and healing, protecting from stressors and exposing to stressors. You may find it helpful to think about wisdom in four different ways – as food and as medicine, as a compass and as a shield.

Wisdom as food

Wisdom food has to taste good or we spit it out. Your children probably hate lectures and monologues, sermons and other forms of gluggy, unappetising wisdom food. So try and make your wisdom food simple and tasty – a crisp little wisdom salad, a little wisdom ice cream for desert. The aim is to develop their capacity to see, deeply and truly, to draw out their understanding- based on this seeing.

Give small helpings. It is easy to let them know in a few words that you understand how they feel about something important; ask them what they think they might do about something – how they would go about it – and in another few words, encourage them to try it, unless it sounds like a total disaster. Later, you can talk about how it went, and help them feel good about their skills and successes, and help them tease out the insights and lessons, and what they might do next time.

Wisdom as medicine

As a parent, or as a teacher, you also need to give wisdom as medicine, to restore well-being when your children are lost or stressed, in some serious pain or difficulty. Alternatively, at some time, your child may be unwise, but feeling terrific. They may be being a bully, or mean or greedy. They may have grown arrogant or rude or dangerous. In this case, you must defeat the unwisdom - the unwise actions and attitudes - and increase your child's wisdom. And defeat, as they say, is a bitter pill to swallow.

It's important to intervene promptly, because unwise behaviour quickly entrenches itself – and often leads to medical or legal problems, which are much harder to solve – or your child grows up the same, into an adult bully, for example.

If your child is just not aware of their behaviour and its effects, you can carefully but directly bring it to their attention and invite them to think about it. The medicine will probably taste of embarrassment mixed with some shame. Once they are able to see for themselves the uncomfortable truth, then, if they have hurt anybody, you should help them say they are sorry, face-to-face, and make amends. Research indicates that this strategy works much better than simply punishing the child in isolation, because they feel the emotional impact of what they have done, and this strengthens their social awareness.

However, if your child is quite aware of what they are doing and don't want to change, just because you say so, then you have just entered into a dominance contest with a younger member of your species. They want to see your power – and they want to test it. Can you defeat them? But you have to defeat them with the power of your conscious loving wisdom. This is a good challenge. You need to realise that defeat is not punishment. It's different. If you just bludgeon them with heavy punishments, or simply squash them with the weight of your authority, then inside themselves, they don't feel that you have been able to meet them, and you lose their respect.

One of Australia's most repugnant murders was of a young woman picked at random for sadistic entertainment. She was raped and strangled by a young man whose mother and step-father had never effectively confronted his unwise power and defeated him, while he was growing up.

Parents must defeat unwise behaviour in their children. Your children want to know that you are wise and powerful – they don't want a parent who is powerful but not wise, and they don't want a parent who is weak. Usually of course, at first you don't know what to do, you are out of your depth. Children force us to grow – and often we don't want to. So you may need to spend a little time and talk to your friends, some other parents, maybe do some reading and thinking, until you gather the wisdom and the power to win the contest, and feel clear and centered in your heart.

If your child is very powerful, for example if they are addicted to alcohol or heroin, then you need to organise overwhelming force, such as a carefully structured group intervention, well supported by professional support services.

Recent figures indicate that these kinds of group interventions, well supported and linked to residential treatment have a success rate of over 80 percent. Wisdom which is medicine can be very powerful, and the dose can be varied. You always use your power to build a strong enough team of friends and experts, to help you succeed.

Wisdom as a compass

Wisdom is also a compass. It provides children with the foundation for their sense of meaning and balance, in their actions and judgments. Children naturally have an intuitive sense of well-being, but only when they can understand how to make wise choices based on the principle of well-being, including the well-being of the whole, can they know where they stand.

Wisdom is a compass because it enables you to get your bearings in a situation, work out where you are and which way you want to go. When your children go out into the shifting and often treacherous social landscape, as adolescents and as young adults, you want them to have that compass. You want them to explore, to have adventures and to be able to safely find their way.

Wisdom as a shield

Wisdom is also a shield. Whenever a situation becomes too dangerous or damaging, or too emotionally distressing, you want your children to be able to act powerfully and quickly to protect themselves – to use their wisdom like a shield. The moment they know that they are not okay they need to be able to find enough wise power to make them safe again.

Your children need people to turn to, and its best if they are people they know and trust very well. Too many children know that they are in trouble, but they are just unable to organise enough wise power to protect themselves. Depression is caused by having too many stressors, too little power to defeat or remove them, and not enough social support to help restore our emotional and biochemical equilibrium – inadequate homeostasis.

Unresolved stress always leads to exhaustion, which is very dangerous, because it leads to fragmented and distorted thinking, and loss of initiative and morale. You want your children to be very clear about how to use wisdom as a shield. Wisdom protects the biochemistry and development of the brain.

When they understand what wisdom is – this open awareness which sees how things happen – and when they learn to search for it, and learn how to find it by gathering together this wise "seeing-power" of people that they know, and developing it in themselves, then this wisdom gives children their own power and freedom. You can teach them how to find it in conversations with other people, and how to create some wisdom by teasing out the elements of something that has happened, all the time developing their own insight.

Wisdom makes your children valuable members of any group, and it builds their self-worth, not on knowledge or games or wealth, but on the real foundation, the Self.

You can give your children this wisdom every day, in your conversations with them, and in the conversations you help them have with others. You can "lead out their soul", the deep meaning of "education".

Wisdom in action forms the basis of morale. We help our children gain this power to act by empowering them. This is the sixth strategy.

Empowering children

But few have spoken of the actual pleasure derived from giving to someone, from creating something, from finishing a task, from offering unexpected help almost invisibly and anonymously.

Paul Wiener

Happiness does not come from doing easy work but from the afterglow of satisfaction that comes after the achievement of a difficult task that demanded our best.

Theodore I. Rubin

They all attain perfection when they find joy in their work.

Bhagavad Gita [The Lord's Song]

True happiness comes from the joy of deeds well done, the zest of creating things new.

Antoine de Saint-Exupéry

One of the strange ironies of humans is that because we have such big brains, we store most of our knowledge in other people's brains. In every social group each person has some specialised area of knowledge. The most important thing we have to know is how to access this knowledge – whose brains hold the knowledge we need right now, and how do we get it out of them. This is social knowledge – and it gives us power.

So, as humans, power comes from two sources – inside yourself, your own knowledge, skills and energy, and outside yourself, primarily from your social supports, the family members, friends and community members whom you know and feel comfortable asking for help. It's crucial to make use of this second source of empowerment – it is always far bigger than our own separate power.

When you look at Tiger Woods, the champion of the world in his chosen sport, did he do it by himself? Of course not. His father deeply regretted having been too busy in the army to have much time to spend with his previous children. He did not want to make that same mistake with Tiger, so he devoted himself to his new son, giving him the power to turn his interest into a passion and his passion into excellence. It was Tiger Woods' dad who nurtured his son's calm prowess – which now inspires and encourages young people around the world. His dad connected him to the coaches and experts who had the knowledge and power to build his skills.

So to empower your children, it's not enough to just build their own power and resourcefulness. You need to carefully weave them into the social fabric of your community and your extended family. Social integration and social supports are the most important protection against depression and suicide. And parents are the main weavers of our social fabric.

We can weave distance, distrust, competitiveness and envy, or we can weave intimacy, trust, cooperation and affection. The cloth we weave, we and our children wear. One of the strongest threads to weave this fabric is reciprocal help.

How do you weave this cloth – and empower children?

You ask people to help your children, and ask people to ask your children to help them. As Hillary Clinton wrote, it takes a village to raise a child. It's very important that each child feels there is a circle of adults who encourage them, enjoy them, nurture and extend them. Encourage your peers to become active elders. Most adults are delighted and honoured by these invitations to share their love and wisdom in a practical way.

You can also make some of your friends into uncles and aunties for your children, and you can adopt an honorary grandpa or grandma if your children's real grandparents are no longer alive. When I was a child, several of my very best uncles and aunts were really just close friends of my parents, even though I had wonderful real aunts and uncles as well. From a child's point of view, the more loving adults who help them, the better.

Develop children's powers to help others

At the same time, create many situations where your children help others. When they learn how to be helpful, they experience in a real way their own worth to other people, and they taste the joy of giving help. They develop the habits of mutual cooperation and at the same time, start to weave their own social fabric and build their social supports.

Depression is a consequence of learnt helplessness. You want to build the opposite – learnt helpfulness. The more cooperative activities your children participate in, where they actively contribute with their skills and energy, the more confident and competent they become. They learn to be powerful, and they earn gratitude and respect, which are the best foundations for status.

Four tips to help you empower children

The three S formula

The first tip is to use the three S formula – **small, soon, successful**. For starters, you want to create a pattern of small wins. When you ask a friend to help your child, try and ask them for something limited that they will be happy to do, something that they are quite capable of doing. Like showing them how to play the first three chords on the guitar. Don't ask for three months of lessons.

Similarly, when you ask someone to ask one of your children to help them, keep it small enough and simple enough for them to do enthusiastically and successfully. Maybe your mother could do with a hand to plant some spring flowers. Maybe your brother could use a hand to paint a fence. Maybe the family next-door is having a children's party soon, and would like some help with the balloons, or running a game.

As much as possible, encourage other people to ask your child directly, even if they have talked about it with you first. In this way, your child feels the respect of being asked for help.

Start this soon, and try to organise activities that happen soon, naturally arising out of day-to-day needs and desires. In this way you create for your children a momentum of successful gifts of help, and an easy emotional flow of desire, asking for help and getting help, hand-in-hand with repeated experiences of being asked for help, willingly giving help, and feeling someone else's gratitude for their generosity and competence.

Make helping fun

The second tip is to make helping fun. Remember that the spirit of play brings work alive, and also, organise some time to share good food, enjoy each other's company and talk about both the achievements and the efforts. You may be surprised at just how much children enjoy doing good work and helping.

In Moree, an outback town in Northern New South Wales, right through the heat of one summer holidays, each Monday morning for four hours about 40 children used to get together to do community cleanups around the houses in their neighbourhood. Their only reward, apart from the fun of working together, was a big barbecue lunch, and their only complaint was that it was so long till next Monday.

The more your children enjoy getting in and working hard, the more they discover their own power to achieve good results and overcome obstacles. Also, they learn how people organise themselves into groups to collectively achieve much more than they could on their own – and enjoy it more. Make this helping work both ways – when your child wants something, and needs help, help them ask for it and organise for it to be fun.

Feed their passion

The third tip is to feed passion and inspiration. Encourage your children to enjoy their passions and inspirations. When the full power of your child's enthusiasm is flowing through them into some activity which is consuming them, then they feel most powerfully alive. In many ways, good parenting is about nurturing and managing these enthusiasms.

Try not to break up their weekends into too many little pieces, but help them follow the energy of their passion until they are naturally tired, and have created the dream that inspired them.

Use consequential learning

The fourth tip is to use consequential learning. Use what? Consequential learning happens when the consequences of what you do teach you to do it better next time. For example, camping is a good activity for children, because if you don't put the tent up right and it rains, you get wet, and if you don't pay attention to the fire your sausages are burnt – or raw. Your children become empowered the more they are able to try things for themselves, and then accept the lessons in the outcome, without being blamed or shamed, and without being able to get themselves off the hook with excuses and red herrings. A burnt sausage pays no attention to any red herring, and children to swallow their pride as they swallow that sausage. But this sort of learning experience actually builds prowess and pride very quickly, because it is very elegant teaching, and highly motivating.

Empowerment is a very specific food to build well-being. Children can be well loved and perfectly happy, and yet have very little experience of using their own power. Children need to be given enough freedom before they will actually act on their own initiative, and not just try to please their parents – or act in a constrained way, like a prisoner who has forgotten how to be free. We only develop free will to the extent that we experience and learn it, so children need to feel their sense of freedom and the surprising urges of their will.

Developing a sense of freedom is very important, because then your children never lose their power to make choices at any point. We do not live in a slave state – just the opposite – we live in a free democracy, and yet for many people, when stresses increase their pressure, they feel powerless to make choices which will remove the stress. Empowerment is always relative, and we live in a very driven society, so your children need a strong sense of their freedom to make wise choices to maintain their well-being, rather than succumb to a sense of helplessness.

The problem is of course that freedom on its own is often a cruel cage – after school, most children are free from imposed activities but many are not free to do almost anything that they really want, everybody whose company they enjoy lives too far away. The fact that lots of children adapt to this doesn't make it a good idea. Raiding the fridge and hanging out with all the lively play-people on television is not empowering.

Doing real things with real people

The more you are able to help your children do real things that they really want to do with other real people the better. For children, the sense of empowerment is very much about their power to create joy with their friends.

Empowerment involves stepping into your power, taking risks and going beyond what you have done before. Just think of Harry Potter – every time you turn the page because you just have to see what amazing thing is about to happen to him – if he's not in trouble at the start of the page, he will be before the end of it! One reason Harry Potter is such a phenomenon is because he keeps developing his power and then going beyond it.

Whenever your children stretch themselves to try something they really want to do, and haven't done before, they feel exhilarated. The more they stretch themselves in this way, the more their power grows in them. You can notice when they get excited about whether they could jump that scary space between where they are now and their dream. If you can encourage them and help them, but not lead them, then they get that wonderful sense of doing it themselves – they feel inspired.

Building morale

*Life owes us little; we owe it everything.
The only true happiness comes from squandering ourselves for a
purpose.*

John Marm Brown

*Many persons have a wrong idea of what constitutes true happiness. It is not attained through self-gratification but through
fidelity to a worthy purpose.*

Helen Keller

Happiness is the sense that one matters.

Sarah Trimmer

*This is the true joy in life – being used for a purpose recognized by
yourself as a mighty one; being thoroughly worn out before you
are thrown on the scrap heap; being a force of nature instead of a
feverish selfish little clod of ailments and grievances, complaining
that the world will not devote itself to making you consistent.*

George Bernard Shaw

GOLFBALLS

A professor walked into his lecture hall carrying a tray. On the tray were a bowl of golf balls, a tin of gravel, a bucket of sand, a large empty jar, and two cans of beer.

Silently, he put the tray on his table and proceeded to fill the jar with golf balls. He held it up to the class.
"Is this full?" he asked.
"Yes," the students replied.
He picked up the tin of gravel and carefully poured it over the golf balls till no more would fit. He held the jar up.
"Is it full?" he asked.
"Yes," they said.
He took the bucket of sand and sprinkled the sand into the jar, shaking the jar so the sand would settle. He held the jar up.
"Is it full?" he asked again.
"Yes," the students answered.
He popped open the two cans of beer and poured them into the jar.
"So what am I teaching you?" he asked.
No-one knew; no-one could answer.
"Well," he said, "the empty jar is your life. The golf balls are the things you really love to do – the most important things. The gravel is the things you have to do to be able to do the really important things. The sand is everything else – all the little things. So always put the golf balls in first. That's my point."
A student asked: "What was the beer for?"
"Oh," said the professor. "That's just to show you that no matter how full your life is, you can always find room for a couple of beers."

The most exciting human games have always been where a group of individuals must cooperate and perform to their best in order to compete with another group for dominance. This is rocket fuel for humans. Adrenaline, glucocorticoids, extra blood sugar – all the good stuff! Warfare, team sports, colonialism and capitalism all run on this. And the morale of the group is the single most important psychological factor.

In order to understand morale, we have to start at the beginning – our evolutionary design. As you know, we are a species of socially organised predacious primates. Our well-being and our survival, and our evolutionary success, depends on the quality and power of our social organisation to hunt for food and resources, and to protect ourselves. From early childhood to old age, every individual member of the social group desires and needs to have an active role in these important socially organised activities.

Because individual survival and success depends on how well the whole group organises itself in this way, each person has a sense of morale which is directly proportional to their confidence in this organised power, and their own involvement and contribution.

Morale is a sense of confidence based in competence and active contribution. Morale is not a nutrient – you can't feed it to your passive children – to get it, they have to participate actively and aggressively to achieve something important for the group. Morale only comes from a sense of intense shared effort, involving discipline and training and learned toughness from some form of contest and struggle. This gladiatorial spirit is not only grown in physical sports like rugby or hockey or netball.

If your child is in a band, or a choir, or in a play, or a good community project – whenever they are part of a group which puts in great efforts together to meet a challenge and achieve an important and worthwhile goal, then they will develop a sense of morale.

The power of synergy

Children who do not participate in these sports and groups often have low morale, and do not learn to understand the inner power that comes through us when we are passionately committed to a struggle to achieve something. They never experience the extraordinary power of synergy when a group puts its hearts and minds together, and they never experience the wonderful exhilaration and camaraderie that come after a group has done its best and triumphed.

Further, it is very hard for them to learn how to be part of the team, how to pull their weight and how to lead. So they don't learn what morale is, and how you build it.

But your children enter the world as automatic members of their most important group, your family – including your extended family. The more you are able to give your children ways to participate in active and important roles, the more you will build their sense of morale.

Very small children love to help doing big things – they like to do things that are right at the outside edge of their ability – they want to help you paint, they want to put the guinea pig back into its cage, they want to carry the eggs from the fridge.

Whenever they sense that something is important to you, they often want to help. This of course, tends to make life a bit exciting and messy for you. Lots of early childhood training is instructions which you give your children while they are helping – "hold that carefully!", "watch where you are going!", "just a little bit of paint!" etc... Bigger children want jobs that are bigger in importance and stretch them – but not bigger in drudgery...

The foundations of morale

It is very useful for you to understand the foundations of morale. There must be a great and noble object to be achieved, and its achievement must be vital. The method of achieving it must be active and aggressive, requiring focus and effort. And the person must feel that what they are and what they do makes a direct contribution towards achieving the goal.

However, they must be convinced that the goal can be achieved – that it is not out of reach or hopeless. Also, they must have confidence that the group they belong to is efficient and well-organised. They must have confidence in the leaders of the group, and know that their own efforts are important and valued. They must feel that they are treated fairly, and get as much help as they need to play their part to the best of their ability.

The primary foundation of morale is always the first one – to be inspired by a great and noble purpose. For millions of poor and dispossessed youth around the world only radical Islam offers them this vision of a great and noble goal. Becoming a great and noble consumer is not inspiring – to anyone.

The Foundations of Morale

Spiritual
1. There must be a great and noble object or purpose.
2. Its achievement must be vital.
3. The method of achievement must be active and aggressive or vigorous.
4. The person must feel that what they are and what they do matters directly towards the attainment of the object.

Intellectual
1. The person must be convinced that the object can be obtained; that it is not out of reach.
2. They must see also that the organisational group to which they belong and which is striving to obtain the object is an efficient one.
3. They must have confidence in the leaders or elders and know that whatever dangers and hardships they are called upon to suffer, their life and efforts will not be dismissed or wasted.

Material
1. The person must feel that they will get a fair deal from the leaders or elders, and from the group or organisation generally.
2. They must, as far as humanly possible, be given the best tools and resources for their task.
3. Their living and working conditions must be made as good as they can be.

Adapted from Sir William Slim

Morale is vital for adolescents

As your children grow, their sense of what is a great and noble object changes. So the challenge for you is to help them find these changing goals which can inspire and motivate them. Morale is an issue which gets more important after adolescence, because your children become more thoughtful and more powerful – and more idealistic. If the only great and noble objects you offer them to contribute to the well-being of the family are doing the dishes and cleaning their rooms their sense of morale will fall. They need bigger and more important challenges. Can they plan a family holiday, or a party for their friends? Can they join in a community project, which they are really passionate about, like building a skateboard ramp in the park, or organising a concert to raise money for a youth project?

One group of teenagers in a small country town raised over $200,000 and got a large community swimming pool built, by determination and creative cooperation. A group of teenagers in another small town established a youth centre – and even got the funding for a permanent youth development worker. Teenagers catch fire and come alive when they can pursue a great and noble object together.

Too many towns – and too many families – exclude and insult their adolescent and older youth, because they don't realise the importance of morale in well-being, and they don't think creatively about how to increase and maintain their sense of morale. Often they treat youth like a Russian bear in a travelling circus – dangerously large muscles and claws, dangerously small brain – and try to cage them with rules and curfews and Paddy wagons.

The trouble is, that it is very easy to demoralise youth and children, it is very easy to exclude them and it is very easy to cage them.

Demoralisation is contagious. If your children are growing up in a community that excludes and demoralises adolescents and youth, it is important to gather some allies and create some strategies and opportunities to increase morale for them and their peers. Usually this age group has very good ideas about what it would like, and if you are able to sit around and encourage them to talk, then you can help them find the power and support to make these goals realities.

Very small groups sitting around talking about increasing the collective well-being are always where community growth and revitalisation begin. And because it is such an active and creative process, building morale is enjoyable and very satisfying – you have a lot of fun doing it.

Protecting a depressed or suicidal child: a systematic strategy

Right up front, let me stress two points.

First, if you think a child may be depressed already, take them to a good doctor, counsellor or psychologist straight away for a careful diagnosis. Early diagnosis and treatment is crucially important in stopping depression taking hold. You can use the strategies in this book to help you identify and remove specific causes of their depression, and directly increase their joy and personal power to create a more satisfying life.

Second, if you think a child may be suicidal, act immediately. Ask them gently but directly if they are feeling suicidal. They will usually tell you. Listen carefully and non-judgementally to what they say. Then, if they are feeling suicidal, act immediately. Talk to at least two health care professionals who are good in this area and recommended by people you trust. Get help to find a key carer, create an intervention plan and organise three support teams.

You can do this in an hour – the same day you find out a child is feeling suicidal. You can do it on one sheet of paper. You can start with one name, one phone number, one idea. You put it into action with your first phone call or conversation.

The point is to act immediately, and build your plan and teams day by day.

If someone told you that there was smoke coming out of the house next door and they thought there was a child inside, you would act instantly, probably with fierce determination – quite possibly with great courage, if courage was needed. Suicide kills more children and young people than house fires. There is no smoke to let you know how big the risk is. My policy is always to act immediately and as powerfully as I can, as soon as I discover that someone is suicidal.

Creating a systematic strategy

It is very common that people are frightened of depression and particularly frightened of suicide. This is completely natural and understandable. However, it can mean that people avoid facing the truth – they choose to overlook symptoms of misery and depression, they downplay both the seriousness and the duration of symptoms and believe that if they ignore the problem it will go away. Sometimes it does – but sometimes it doesn't, and in very many cases when a child commits suicide, parents and other adults knew that the child had been unhappy – but had not known what to do. This is a tragedy of ignorance and fear. It is far better take the symptoms seriously right from the start and to create a systematic strategy from the very beginning.

As well as avoiding facing the truth, because of this fear, it is common for people to want the problem to go away fast. So treatment, if any, is often too little, begun late and ended far too soon. We want a depressed child to "just snap out of it". We would just like there to be a magic pill. There isn't.

Chronic depression is the most serious and dangerous child-hood condition. Mental agony makes people want to die. Far too many cases of depression are merely treated at the time of crisis. Even if the crisis treatment apparently works, it is often like putting a patch on a bald tire: the situation has gone beyond a simple patch. Depressed people are at their greatest risk of suicide in the month immediately after they have been given crisis treatment in a mental ward.

So whether a child is depressed or suicidal, you need to make a comprehensive and systematic strategy – not a series of Band-Aids. A systematic strategy includes selecting a key carer, creating support teams, getting a high-quality diagnosis from expert professionals, creating an intervention plan with suffi-cient speed and power to protect and heal the child, and using and adapting the strategies in this book to increase the flow of nutrients to the child, increase the strength of the social fabric around them and develop the child's own resilience and morale.

Be in a rush to get started, be very determined to defeat the depression, and prevent suicide, but take the time to really build solid foundations of well-being and morale. Remember that a comprehensive and systematic strategy is a long series of experiments, and the more creative and attentive you are, the faster you see what works and learn how to restore shim-mering well-being.

The key carer

Who loves and cares most passionately for the well-being of this child? This person usually makes the best key carer. It may be you; it may be the couple who are the parents; it may be a friend or a family member. It is very important to find a key carer – that person who will dedicate themselves single-mindedly to running the protection, nurturing and healing of the suicidal child. But the safety and well-being of the child depend very much on the key carer's confidence, power and endurance – they need a support team.

The first support team

The first support team is the team for the person who is the key carer. If you are the key carer, create your support team fast and simply by asking your best and most effective friends if they will help. You can grow your support team naturally as you find other people who can help. This support team provides vital intimate friendship, shoulders to cry on, ideas and practical help, meals, visits and outings, etc. it provides love, joy, and above all, power.

The key rule is to never burn out any member of your team. You need them to feel okay about what they give, so be very sensitive about what you ask anyone to do. Make this support team big enough so that each person only gives a little bit, and is happy to be part of the team.

The second support team

The second support team is made up of the best available health professionals, and you can grow this team as you hear of very good professional people and talk to them. Bureaucracies naturally contain people of widely varying abilities and commitment. The difference between a brilliant professional and an ordinary one is not 10 or 15% – much more like thousands of percent!! Be polite to every health professional, and continually hunt for the best. They can often make the difference – quite literally – between life and death. For example, one skilled health professional was able to persuade a young person with schizophrenia to take their daily antipsychotic medication, whereas another professional, equally highly qualified, failed completely. Only the medication, which prevents psychotic episodes, enables the family to care for their young adult with a serious mental illness during the crucial early period where the person learns to adapt to their own unexpected and completely unwanted disability. Taking the medication regularly is also vital to protect the brain from the damage caused by further psychotic episodes.

In a second example, a brilliant and very experienced child and adolescent psychologist, who looks much more like a cowherd than a clinician, effortlessly extracted a genuine promise not to commit suicide from a 14-year-old boy, who had up to then defied all professional attempts to end his determination to commit suicide. This promise alone made it possible to develop and implement a long and successful intervention plan.

You should speak personally to each of these professionals and you should keep their phone numbers with you. You particularly need to know beforehand who to call and how to get the right professional help at 2 a.m. on a Saturday morning or four o'clock on a Sunday afternoon. You also need to know from your professional team how and where to get a reliable hospitalisation in an emergency. The key point is to make it *your* professional support team – known personally by you and the child, and happily committed to giving you their best.

The third support team

The third support team is to provide ongoing emotional support for the suicidal child. This can include the child's close friends and relatives. It may include those best available professionals who are good at talking to the child as well as close friends and family who can give time and attentive care. The key carer and family can create opportunities for the child and their friends to do good things together, including work and other contributions, have adventures, play games, etc. the aim is to increase the flow of joyful experiences, strengthen these friendships and restore a sense of confidence and morale.

Creating an intervention plan

The first two basic principles of suicide prevention are overwhelming force and overwhelming speed.

This does not mean shock and awe, neither blitzkrieg nor the bombing of Baghdad. This overwhelming force consists of people who together have love, compassion, time, attention and skill, but they must also be organised, determined and serious – more powerful than the power of the person who is suicidal – and they must be able to act faster than that person. For example, if someone is suicidal it is important not to leave them alone. The three most risky times are the six hours after a person has become drunk, the first two weeks after the loss of an important relationship or a shameful experience such as failure or defeat, and the first 30 days after a person has been released from hospital or crisis centre after being treated for a psychiatric condition. Clearly it takes a committed team of people who can each put in a little time, to provide this powerful intervention and companionship. Never be afraid of acting powerfully to prevent suicide. Many people lose a child to suicide because they afraid of acting powerfully – and then their lives are filled with the power of grief, regrets, guilt or doubt forever after.

The intervention plan includes creating the three support teams, organising for those teams to stay very close around the suicidal child, in a respectful and loving manner, and getting regular professional counselling and treatment in place immediately.

In a nutshell, the aim of the plan is to create a living containment vessel around the suicidal child, which can contain their unwise behaviour for a period of time, and restore their strong desire to live. The key carer must make sure that they and the teams pay very close attention, watching the child's well-being and sharing observations, hunches and ideas. As well as creating and maintaining this field of consciousness around the child, the key carer and teams must be pro-active and creative – not simply reactive. They need to anticipate what the child may need and do next, and they need to continuously co-create ideas and activities to build well-being and happiness. Every activity is just an experiment – and the more things you try the faster you will learn about how to nurture well-being and empower the child.

The third basic principle of suicide prevention is to create an intervention plan which is comprehensive and long-term.

This means that an intervention plan should also include helping the child defeat all the problems which led to their distress, and accept and process any unavoidable losses or defeats, such as the end of a relationship. Finally, the intervention plan should systematically strengthen the well-being of the child, their fabric of strong positive relationships and their ability to create happiness. This book contains many ideas to strengthen children's well-being.

It is vital to recognise, right from the start, that mental health services **only** provide short-term crisis accommodation, and only if they have the beds available. Often it is the shock and trauma of crisis treatment which precipitates suicide.

This means that the support teams and family need to take responsibility right from the start for creating the comprehensive and long-term aspects of the plan, and organise powerful enough teams to make this possible and successful.

If someone is suicidal, you have to create a plan and support teams strong enough to protect the suicidal person and help them grow their own wisdom and support over a period of time, and you have to act much faster than they do. People, including teenagers, when they are suicidal can become very determined, very devious in denying and concealing their plans, and very impulsive, capable of acting very fast. You should always take suicidal thoughts and feelings completely seriously.

If you act with overwhelming speed to create the support teams and the plan which is powerful enough to prevent suicide, then you can act calmly and gently to heal the distress and restore well-being, as best you can, because you are prepared. If it turns out that the crisis fades away or reveals itself to have been quite minor, this is wonderful. But the preparation will not be wasted, because it will increase your speed and skills, and it is likely that some time in the future you will be able to help someone who is suicidal or someone who is caring for a person who is suicidal. Being prepared, powerfully and rapidly, will increase the quality of your attentiveness and your insight, and will help you to be more courageous and creative in exploring how to nurture immediate and long-term well-being. The strategies and knowledge contained in this book will help you restore and strengthen well-being in children who are depressed or suicidal.

HIGH PARENT MORALE – LOW CHILD MORALE

A COMMON TRAP FOR PARENTS

Often parents have high morale and therefore have lower needs for joy, love or wisdom.

Their morale is high because they are creating and managing a family. They have a great and noble purpose, a vital role, and a lot of power. They also may have a job and career.

They assume that their children share in their high sense of meaning and morale, but often the children do not. So the children have much higher needs for joy, love, wisdom and empowerment than the parents recognise or provide.

Also, the children may have a very low or fragile sense of morale, which the parents do not realise. It is not uncommon for children to feel as though they live in an emotional desert, while their parents' lives feel rich and meaningful.

<u>Mental Well-Being and Health</u>:
things your children need

1. Frequent regular experiences of happiness

2. Frequent regular periods of no stress

3. Frequent loving connections with known friends and elders

4. A source of wisdom and fair moral regulation

5. A sense of personal freedom, power and inspiration

6. High morale

7. A strong sense of purpose

8. Active worthwhile roles

9. Membership of at least one strong social group

Conclusion

We will never eradicate depression. It is built into our biochemistry and linked to the genetic mechanisms of dominance. It is very important that if you think any of your children are showing signs of depression or mental illness, that you seek prompt medical advice and create a systematic strategy.

You might well ask why is dominance necessary? Is it avoidable? The answer is that it is necessary and unavoidable. The explanation is found in the two fundamental laws of genetics which Gregor Mendel discovered. Gregor Mendel was a 19th-century monk, who was also a scientist, fascinated by plant genetics. He discovered that genes are either dominant or recessive and they do not ever blend. Second, he discovered that the mixture of dominant and recessive genes present in each individual in each generation is completely random. This means that in every human group, the individuals born in each generation have a unique genetic make-up.

Natural selection requires that the fittest of these individuals must take genetic dominance to maximise the adaptive success of the group – its well-being in future generations is based on this natural dominance competition.

Human groups and cultures have always established codes of law and norms of behaviour to try and regulate – and often manipulate this innate dominance behaviour. It is ironic that at the same time that Gregor Mendel was tending his peas in the monastery garden in Moravia, Karl Marx was working furiously to design a unique global system to try and over rules human dominance. When the Berlin Wall crashed down in 1989, the gentle scientist established complete domination over the formidable philosopher. At the genetic heart of evolution, there will always be the same necessary violent collisions as in all chemical reactions.

But you can protect your children from developing clinical depression using these seven strategies.

First, you can understand depression.

Second, you can understand the five elements of human well-being – the nutrients of Joy, Love and connection, wisdom and empowerment, and morale.

Third, you can increase the flow of joy.

Fourth, you can increase the flow of love and connection.

Fifth, you can organise the transmission of wisdom.

Sixth, you can empower your children.

And **seventh**, you can build their morale.

These seven strategies offer you a clear and simple framework to assist you as a parent. They can help you sort out your children's current needs and search for any obvious deficiencies. They can help you create a richer and more satisfying environment to nurture and strengthen your children's well-being. You and your children will already have literally hundreds of great ideas and skills, things you love to do, and people who care about you deeply.

Putting it all together

These strategies fit together, like all the ingredients in a curry. You can help your children put together days that are magical. And you can mix in a blend of strategies into each week so that the week nourishes your entire family. You can see at a glance when a dog, or a horse is well nourished – it looks sleek and its coat shines. You can see when children's spirits are well-nourished – their faces shine and they have a sense of what they want to do next.

You can use this set of strategies to help you clarify what your intentions are, hidden inside your habitual family activities. They can then help you break free of the external focus, and let you watch and shape what you or your children really want to create. The strategies will also help you to talk with your partner and with your children about your differing senses of how things are going, what things are going well, and what doesn't feel good.

Your family and community can be an environment which inspires continuous shared creativity, where people enjoy each other and give each other support.

You are the key

As the parent, you are the key. You have more power than anyone else to nurture your children and make them shine. **So how do you nurture yourself and your partner?**

Parenting takes you to the end of your tether and then demands more. It takes you out of your depth and then shifts the shore. Being a parent and creating a family are most likely to be the biggest game you will play in your whole life. It will grow you more than any other thing, if you can let it.

Some parents live in a state of almost perpetual agony, some – usually, but not always, the men – run for cover. Some are able to surrender themselves to parenting and having a family, with a level of employment as well, and in this wholehearted choosing, achieve a grace and a creative freedom that brings them daily joy and satisfaction.

Who do you know who parents like this? Can you settle deeply into yourself and feel a peace inside yourself at your choice and your given circumstances? Take a moment now to focus inwards and find this centre and ground.

Centre and ground

The person who is centred and grounded can work with emotional children and difficult family situations without harm.

Being centred means having the ability to recover your balance, even in the midst of action. When you are centred, you are not thrown by sudden excitements or demands. Being grounded means being down to earth, having gravity or weight. I know where I stand, and I know what I stand for: that is ground.

The centred and grounded person has stability and a sense of self. When you are not stable you can easily get carried away by the intensity of parenting or teaching and make mistakes of judgement, or even become ill. When you are centred and grounded your awareness becomes clearer and more sensitive.

The wise parent or teacher pays respectful attention to all behaviour. In this way the children become open to more possibilities of behaviour. They learn a great deal when they are open to everything and not just figuring out what pleases you. (Adapted from *The Tao of Leadership*, by John Heider)

It is easy to be overtaken by a kind of dizzy synergy with children and the other partner, winding each other up until you are all ungrounded and uncentred – a living labyrinth of agitated thoughts and feelings. At this point, someone usually drops some big guilt and punishment bombs, and everyone is left with silent bad feelings, like chemical residue.

In you is a place of living stillness and there you will find, often, your own quiet wisdom, the threads of intuition and sparkles of inspiration which together will shine light on any complex problem and lead you to the strands of a good solution. Around you are so many undiscovered friends, allies, people with whom you can exchange skills and power and good times which nurture you and all your children.

The oldest science

Culture is the oldest human science, and the most important, because it always focuses squarely on the best way to maintain the well-being of the whole social group, working to adapt to each new difficulty, including the difficult, unpredictable collisions of dominance, creating and modifying and transmitting the skills and knowledge to each new child.

I was told the story once about an old aboriginal elder, living on his traditional tribal lands southeast of Darwin, who was asked to explain well-being.

He said, "A man living with people that he loves, he's like a man standing on one leg. He's standing up all right, but he doesn't have much balance. He can fall any way. A man living with people that he loves, in country that he loves, he's like a man standing on two legs. He's stable, but he can still go backwards. A man living with people that he loves, in country that he loves, doing work that he loves, he's like a kangaroo. He can only go forwards."

Appendix

Basic brain facts

As a parent, teacher or counsellor, the better you understand the nature and evolution of the brain, the better you will be able to protect a child from depression.

So the first thing you need to know is that the parts of the brain are usually named for what they look like or where they are.

Even though the brain is far from being completely described, all the names and locating adjectives still come from Latin.

The architecture of the brain is organised in two different ways. The outer part of the brain, the neocortex, is organised in regular layers of different kinds of brain cells. The inner parts of the brain contain hundreds of nuclei, which are brain cells clustered together like bunches of grapes. Often these nuclei are themselves clustered together, like peas in a pod, or sections in an orange.

Many of these nuclei act like glands, secreting different kinds of neurotransmitters. There are over eighty different neurotransmitter chemicals. So the brain is not so much like a computer, running calculations using electricity. Rather it is a hugely complex mixture of glands and layered neurons. It is powered by electrochemical reactions which can rapidly

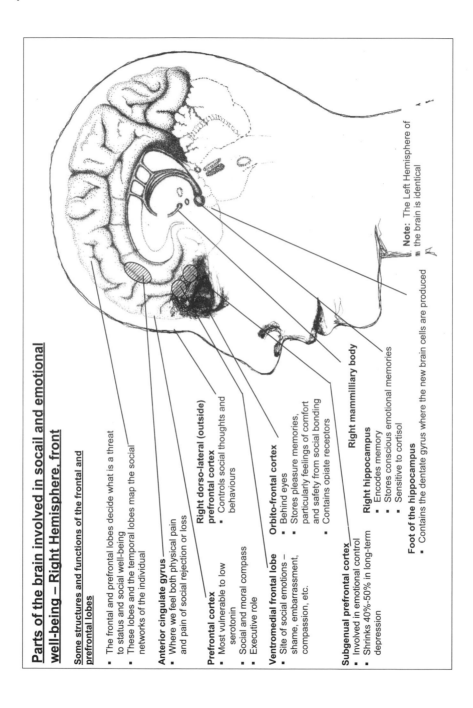

Parts of the brain involved in social and emotional well-being – Right Hemisphere, front

Some structures and functions of the frontal and prefrontal lobes

- The frontal and prefrontal lobes decide what is a threat to status and social well-being
- These lobes and the temporal lobes map the social networks of the individual

Anterior cingulate gyrus
- Where we feel both physical pain and pain of social rejection or loss

Prefrontal cortex
- Most vulnerable to low serotonin
- Social and moral compass
- Executive role

Right dorso-lateral (outside) prefrontal cortex
- Controls social thoughts and behaviours

Ventromedial frontal lobe
- Site of social emotions – shame, embarrassment, compassion, etc.

Orbito-frontal cortex
- Behind eyes
- Stores pleasure memories, particularly feelings of comfort and safety from social bonding
- Contains opiate receptors

Subgenual prefrontal cortex
- Involved in emotional control
- Shrinks 40%-50% in long-term depression

Right mammilliary body

Right hippocampus
- Encodes memory
- Stores conscious emotional memories
- Sensitive to cortisol

Foot of the hippocampus
- Contains the dentate gyrus where the new brain cells are produced

Note: The Left Hemisphere of the brain is identical

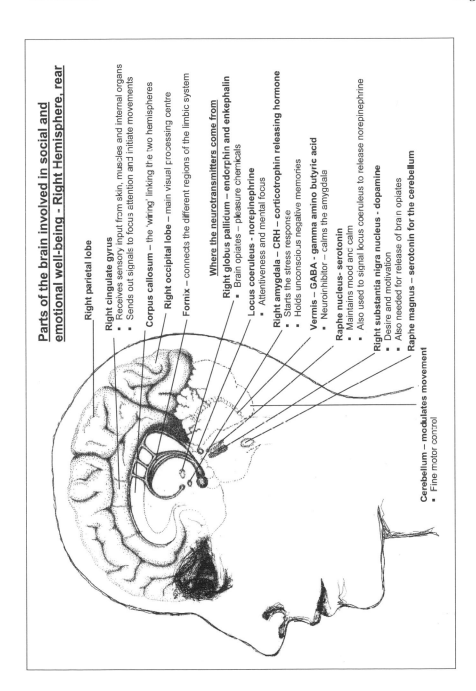

Parts of the brain involved in social and emotional well-being - Right Hemisphere, rear

Right parietal lobe

Right cingulate gyrus
- Receives sensory input from skin, muscles and internal organs
- Sends out signals to focus attention and initiate movements

Corpus callosum – the 'wiring' linking the two hemispheres

Right occipital lobe – main visual processing centre

Fornix – connects the different regions of the limbic system

Where the neurotransmitters come from

Right globus pallidum – endorphin and enkephalin
- Brain opiates – pleasure chemicals

Locus coeruleus - norepinephrine
- Attentiveness and mental focus

Right amygdala – CRH – corticotrophin releasing hormone
- Starts the stress response
- Holds unconscious negative memories

Vermis – GABA - gamma amino butyric acid
- Neuroinhibitor – calms the amygdala

Raphe nucleus- serotonin
- Maintains mood and calm
- Also used to signal locus coeruleus to release norepinephrine

Right substantia nigra nucleus - dopamine
- Desire and motivation
- Also needed for release of brain opiates

Raphe magnus – serotonin for the cerebellum

Cerebellum – modulates movement
- Fine motor control

change both their own chemistry and these structures of the brain, as the external social cues and the internal emotions and thoughts change. When you count up all these nuclei, there may be over 1000 different organs or parts in the brain.

Whenever the brain is under pressure, it changes its fuel mix – the blend of neurotransmitters.

Another important fact is that our brain is not a stand-alone, independent thinking organ. Instead it is inherently interdependent and social. All primates have brains which are highly socially adapted. Humans are the most socially interdependent primate species and our brains are evolved to work best in a stable social group of around 150 people.

Our thinking, our perception, and our memory are inherently both emotional and social. Our moods, our motivation and our mental health are inextricably linked to the quality, security and meaning of our social context. Our brains are adapted to read social cues such as facial expressions, tone of voice and patterns of behaviour. We react most powerfully to any threat to our status in the group. We make "**social maps**" in our brain to keep precise track of the social fabric, and to protect and advance our own dominance in the group.

Continuous signals from the social group to the brain provide a continuous backdrop for the mind. The way we perceive and interpret of these signals dominates both our background mood and our conscious attention. Research shows that when we receive even fleeting friendly signals from others around us, we relax, we express our desires more easily, we even judge food to taste sweeter.

The brain creates and continuously upgrades these "**social maps**". The brain then generates emotional reactions to how it

<u>NEUROTRANSMITTERS</u>

The brain uses both electrical charges and chemical fuels to operate.   It may have over 100 different chemical neurotransmitters. **It has a fuel injection system,** delivering several neurotransmitters to specific areas of the brain via tiny microtubules which also form the structure of each cell.   These neurotransmitters can be stored and reused, or they can be broken down.

Whenever the brain senses or imagines that circumstances have changed, the brain changes the fuel mix and this changes what the brain perceives and how it thinks and feels.

The human brain is particularly tuned to respond to any change in the social context.   Even tiny changes can produce huge changes in these neurotransmitter mixtures.

So, for example, a contemptuous glance of half a second from a peer can flood us with rage, shame or despair.   On the other hand, a tiny half-smile from a close friend can instantly melt our tension and restore confidence – and a tiny half-smile from someone we desire can flood us with joy.

During adolescence, the brain grows extensive new connections between the frontal and prefrontal lobes, and the limbic system, particularly the caudate nuclei.   These connections act as feedback loops to bring more precision and subtlety to this powerful brain chemistry.

The brain is socially constructed.   Brain chemistry and function are affected and regulated by signals transmitted from other people. Ants are socially organised by chemical signals laid down on the ground. We are socially organised by visual (body language, etc) and verbal signals which directly change our neurotransmitter chemical mix.

perceives and imagines these relationships are going between the self and the group.

However we can completely bypass these signals from the group, and directly change these social maps in the brain. So, under stress or depression, the amygdala or the prefrontal cortex, two parts of the brain which are explained shortly, can change the maps directly. Suddenly friends become enemies, lovers become aloof or treacherous, and safe and welcoming situations can appear too dangerous and painful to contemplate. Our thoughts and emotions have the power to transform our reality, and this changes what we do and what happens in our lives.

Structurally, the brain is divided into two hemispheres which are visually similar, but have different functions. The outer covering of each hemisphere, the wrinkled neocortex, is divided into five distinct lobes, separated by valleys, called sulci. From the front of the brain the lobes are: the prefrontal lobes, the frontal lobes, the parietal lobes, the occipital lobes, and at the side, the temporal lobes.

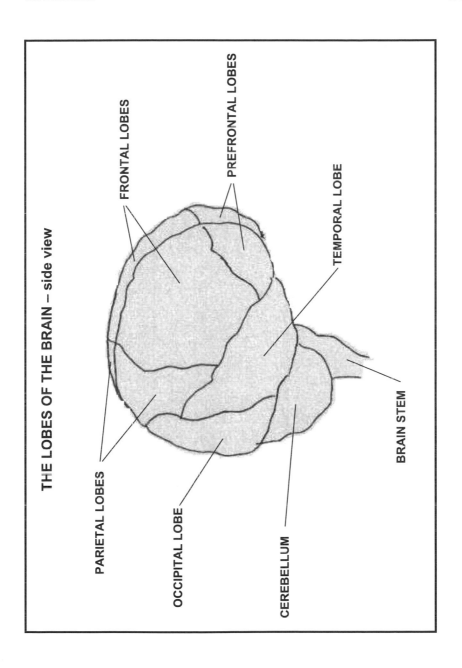

THE LOBES OF THE BRAIN – side view

FRONTAL LOBES

PREFRONTAL LOBES

PARIETAL LOBES

OCCIPITAL LOBE

TEMPORAL LOBE

BRAIN STEM

CEREBELLUM

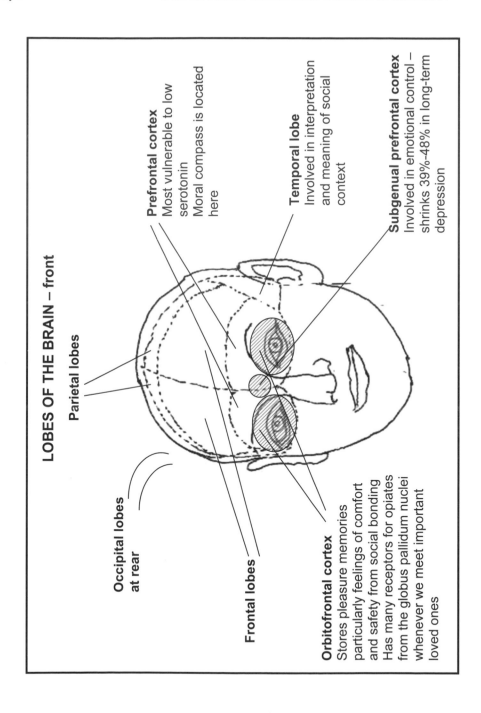

LOBES OF THE BRAIN – front

Parietal lobes

Occipital lobes at rear

Frontal lobes

Prefrontal cortex
Most vulnerable to low serotonin
Moral compass is located here

Temporal lobe
Involved in interpretation and meaning of social context

Subgenual prefrontal cortex
Involved in emotional control – shrinks 39%–48% in long-term depression

Orbitofrontal cortex
Stores pleasure memories particularly feelings of comfort and safety from social bonding
Has many receptors for opiates from the globus pallidum nuclei whenever we meet important loved ones

At the centre of the brain lies the **limbic system**, made up of two visually symmetrical sets of nuclei. The limbic system controls the level of arousal, and the overriding emotional states of the person, including fight or flight, fear and sadness. It also creates and stores the powerful emotional memories. Conscious memories are formed in each *hippocampus*. The *hippocampi*, from the Latin word for seahorse, were so named because they looked like little seahorses to early anatomists.

Powerful unconscious memories are created in the amygdala, which are two almond-shaped clusters of nuclei that scan all sensory inputs from eyes, ears, nose and skin, etc, as well as scanning thoughts generated in the prefrontal lobes, the frontal lobes and the temporal lobes. They play a major role in protecting the person from all threats.

When they sense a threat, the amygdala start the stress reaction, and each hippocampus reacts strongly to cortisol, the main stress hormone. The limbic system not only controls stress and mood, it also distributes the pleasure chemicals, the brain opiates called endorphins and enkephalins.

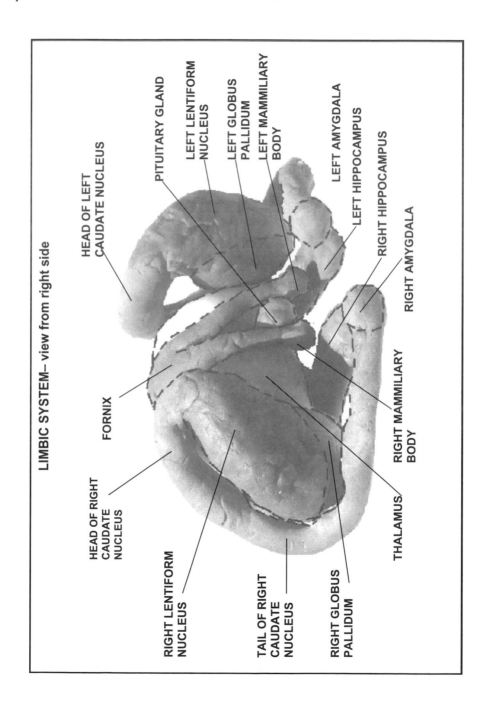

LIMBIC SYSTEM– view from right side

PITUITARY GLAND

HEAD OF LEFT
CAUDATE NUCLEUS

LEFT LENTIFORM
NUCLEUS

LEFT GLOBUS
PALLIDUM

LEFT MAMMILIARY
BODY

LEFT AMYGDALA

LEFT HIPPOCAMPUS

RIGHT HIPPOCAMPUS

RIGHT AMYGDALA

FORNIX

RIGHT MAMMILIARY
BODY

THALAMUS

HEAD OF RIGHT
CAUDATE
NUCLEUS

RIGHT LENTIFORM
NUCLEUS

TAIL OF RIGHT
CAUDATE
NUCLEUS

RIGHT GLOBUS
PALLIDUM

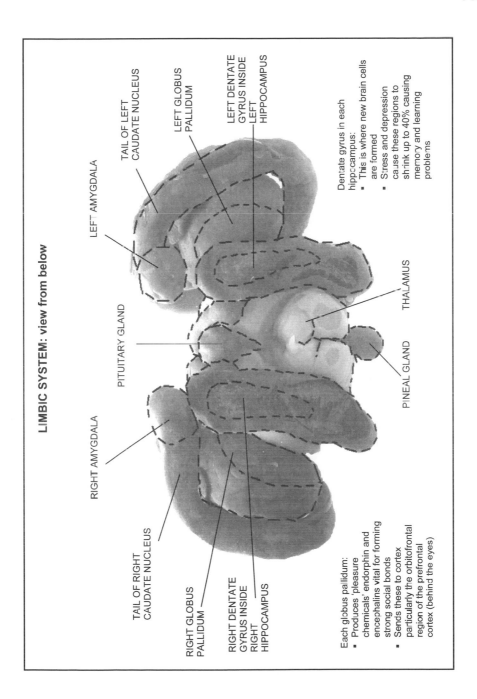

LIMBIC SYSTEM: view from below

RIGHT AMYGDALA

LEFT AMYGDALA

TAIL OF LEFT
CAUDATE NUCLEUS

LEFT GLOBUS
PALLIDUM

LEFT DENTATE
GYRUS INSIDE
LEFT
HIPPOCAMPUS

Dentate gyrus in each
hippocampus:
- This is where new brain cells
  are formed
- Stress and depression
  cause these regions to
  shrink up to 40% causing
  memory and learning
  problems

PITUITARY GLAND

THALAMUS

PINEAL GLAND

TAIL OF RIGHT
CAUDATE NUCLEUS

RIGHT GLOBUS
PALLIDUM

RIGHT DENTATE
GYRUS INSIDE
RIGHT
HIPPOCAMPUS

Each globus pallidum:
- Produces 'pleasure
  chemicals' endorphin and
  encephalins vital for forming
  strong social bonds
- Sends these to cortex
  particularly the orbitofrontal
  region of the prefrontal
  cortex (behind the eyes)

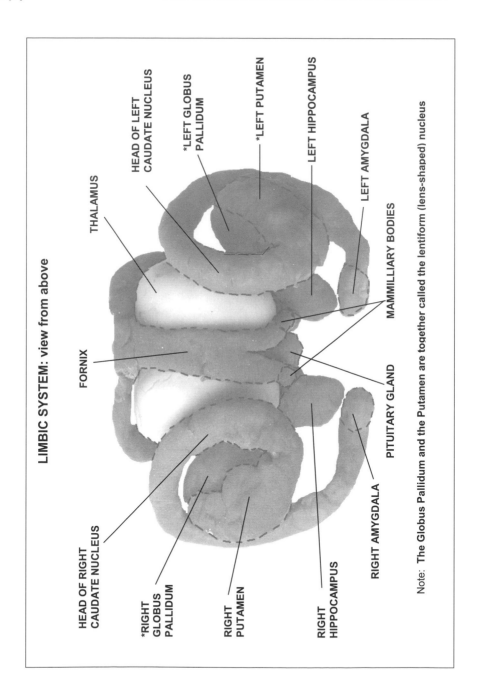

LIMBIC SYSTEM: view from above

HEAD OF RIGHT
CAUDATE NUCLEUS

*RIGHT
GLOBUS
PALLIDUM

RIGHT
PUTAMEN

RIGHT
HIPPOCAMPUS

RIGHT AMYGDALA

PITUITARY GLAND

MAMMILLIARY BODIES

LEFT AMYGDALA

LEFT HIPPOCAMPUS

*LEFT PUTAMEN

*LEFT GLOBUS
PALLIDUM

HEAD OF LEFT
CAUDATE NUCLEUS

THALAMUS

FORNIX

Note: The Globus Pallidum and the Putamen are together called the lentiform (lens-shaped) nucleus

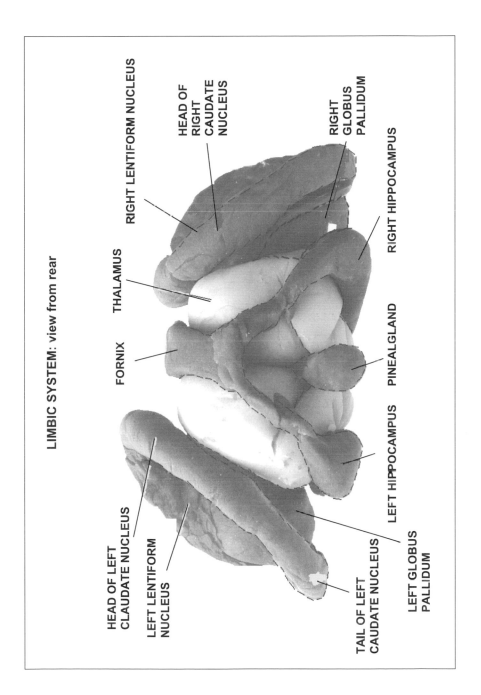

LIMBIC SYSTEM: view from rear

HEAD OF LEFT CLAUDATE NUCLEUS

LEFT LENTIFORM NUCLEUS

HEAD OF RIGHT CAUDATE NUCLEUS

RIGHT LENTIFORM NUCLEUS

RIGHT GLOBUS PALLIDUM

RIGHT HIPPOCAMPUS

THALAMUS

FORNIX

PINEAL GLAND

LEFT HIPPOCAMPUS

TAIL OF LEFT CAUDATE NUCLEUS

LEFT GLOBUS PALLIDUM

Where neurotransmitters come from

Immediately under the limbic system, lie the nuclei which produce the main neurotransmitters involved in depression. Dopamine, which controls motivation, comes from the two substantia nigra, literally the "black substance", nuclei, and from the ventral tegmental nuclei which lie between them. Serotonin, which regulates mood, is produced in the dorsal raphe nucleus and the raphe magnus nucleus. Norepinephirine, which enhances mental focus, is produced in a nucleus called the locus coeruleus. It is an important neurotransmitter during stress, and can signal the amygdala to organise more cortisol from the adrenal cortex glands on the top of the kidneys.

Finally, at the back of the brain lies the cerebellum, which is involved in fine motor coordination. The cerebellum has a layered architecture, with some nuclei at its centre. It has two hemispheres, like a miniature cortex. Lying vertically between these two hemispheres of the cerebellum is a wormlike structure called the vermis. The vermis produces a very important neuroinhibitor called GABA. GABA calms and regulates the limbic system. In particular, it makes the amygdala less reactive to stress, less fearful and less aggressive. If a child is neglected or abused in early childhood this causes the vermis to adapt to a more dangerous social world by permanently reducing its GABA production. These children of abuse or neglect are often more aggressive and reactive. Schizophrenia can also cause these changes to the vermis.

DEPRESSION'S EFFECTS

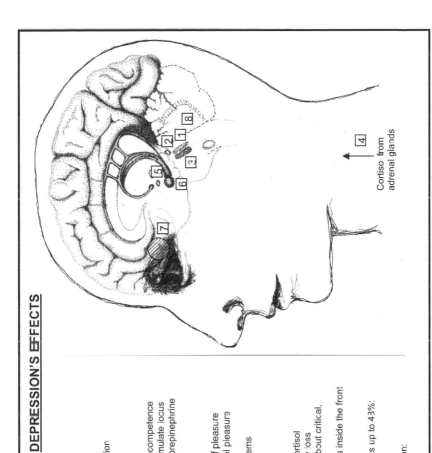

Cortisol from adrenal glands

Changes to biochemistry:

1. Serotonin depletion:
   - Lowered mood
   - Increased impulsiveness and aggression
   - Reduced prefrontal cortex function

2. Norepinephrine depletion:
   - Loss of attentiveness and focus
   - Norepinephrine used up in stressful incompetence
   - Low serotonin means brain cannot stimulate locus coeruleus nucleus to produce more norepinephrine

3. Dopamine depletion:
   - Prolonged stress depletes dopamine
   - Lowered motivation and arousal
   - Dopamine is involved in the release of pleasure neurotransmitters so it is harder to feel pleasure

4. Raised cortisol levels:
   - Damage to many brain and body systems

Changes to brain structure

5. Each hippocampus shrinks:
   - Up to 30% cell loss due to action of cortisol
   - Impairs new learning, causes memory loss
   - Reduced ability to think, particularly about critical, stress-inducing events

6. Loss of new brain cells from dentate gyrus inside the front of each hippocampus:
   - Impaired learning

7. Area of subgenual prefrontal cortex shrinks up to 43%:
   - Reduced emotional control
   - Increased mood swings

8. Vermis may lose part of its GABA secretion:
   - Reduced ability of brain to calm itself

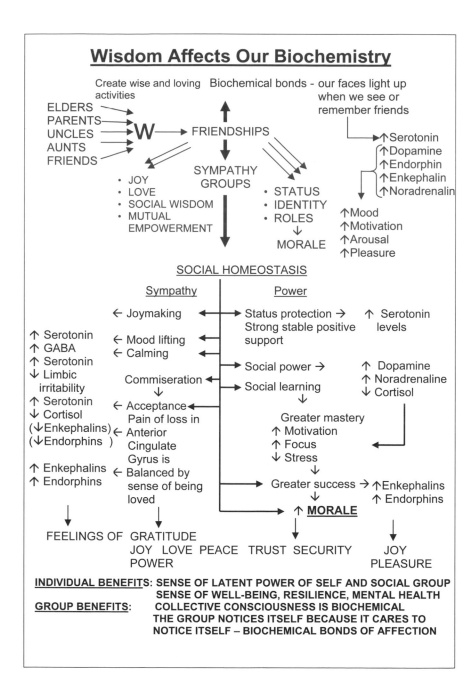

Wisdom Affects Our Biochemistry

Create wise and loving activities   Biochemical bonds - our faces light up when we see or remember friends

ELDERS
PARENTS
UNCLES → **W** → FRIENDSHIPS
AUNTS
FRIENDS

SYMPATHY
GROUPS

- JOY
- LOVE
- SOCIAL WISDOM
- MUTUAL EMPOWERMENT

- STATUS
- IDENTITY
- ROLES
  ↓
  MORALE

↑Serotonin
↑Dopamine
↑Endorphin
↑Enkephalin
↑Noradrenalin

↑Mood
↑Motivation
↑Arousal
↑Pleasure

SOCIAL HOMEOSTASIS

Sympathy   Power

↑ Serotonin   ← Joymaking   ←→ Status protection →   ↑ Serotonin
↑ GABA   Strong stable positive   levels
↑ Serotonin   ← Mood lifting   support
↓ Limbic   ← Calming
irritability   → Social power →   ↑ Dopamine
↑ Serotonin   Commiseration   ↑ Noradrenaline
↓ Cortisol   ↓   → Social learning   ↓ Cortisol
(↓Enkephalins) ← Acceptance ←   ↓
(↓Endorphins) Pain of loss in
               ← Anterior   Greater mastery
               Cingulate   ↑ Motivation
↑ Enkephalins Gyrus is   ↑ Focus
↑ Endorphins   ← Balanced by   ↓ Stress
               sense of being   ↓
               loved   →   Greater success → ↑Enkephalins
                                          ↓   ↑ Endorphins
                                     ↑ **MORALE**

FEELINGS OF GRATITUDE
             JOY LOVE PEACE TRUST SECURITY   JOY
             POWER   PLEASURE

<u>INDIVIDUAL BENEFITS</u>: **SENSE OF LATENT POWER OF SELF AND SOCIAL GROUP
                    SENSE OF WELL-BEING, RESILIENCE, MENTAL HEALTH**
<u>GROUP BENEFITS</u>:   **COLLECTIVE CONSCIOUSNESS IS BIOCHEMICAL
                    THE GROUP NOTICES ITSELF BECAUSE IT CARES TO
                    NOTICE ITSELF – BIOCHEMICAL BONDS OF AFFECTION**

CONCEPT: TENSEGRITY

Tensegrity is a concept developed in civil engineering. A structure is said to have tensegrity when stress at any point causes the structure to realign itself so that the stress is distributed equally. A **GEODESIC DOME** is an example. **Tensegrity** is a special quality of structural flexibility and adaptability. It requires a non-rigid structure composed of rods and cables or tensile materials assembled with flexible connections. The concept has also been applied in cellular biology to explain the structure of cells.

Here we can apply the concept of tensegrity to human social groups, particularly sympathy groups. In a healthy social group, each person's mental health and happiness is maintained by the way their sympathy group adapts and aligns its attention and its organisation to share each stress, provide support and restore mood and status.

Tensegrity requires people in the group to be emotionally well connected, flexible and attentive to each other's social and emotional experiences. Sympathy must be reciprocal and fair. As in a good extended family, when the social bonds are strong and people care about each other, the whole group will pull together to assist and support any member in distress. **As a parent, you can help build this flexible structure of caring connections into your family and your community.**

NEUROTRANSMITTERS INVOLVED IN DEPRESSION (1)

Serotonin

- Regulates mood
- Level of serotonin drops when status or social integration drops
- Regulates calm
- Lowered serotonin leads to increased impulsiveness and aggression
- The stress hormone cortisol reduces serotonin levels
- Serotonin is very important to the functioning of the prefrontal cortex
- Serotonin depletion reduces the production of norepinephrine

Dopamine

- Responsible for desire and motivation
- Level of dopamine drops when the brain judges the person is defeated or exhausted
- Dopamine supply increases during stress but is soon used up
- Most drugs work by putting more dopamine into the synapses

Norepinephrine

- Neurotransmitter released by fear
- Responsible for increased focus and attentiveness
- Supply increases during stress but is soon used up
- Low levels of norepinephrine contribute to depression in many people

NEUROTRANSMITTERS INVOLVED IN DEPRESSION (2)

GABA (gamma-aminobutyric acid)

- A neuroinhibitor, GABA raises the firing threshold of the amygdala neurones, making the limbic system less reactive to threats
- Chronic stress damages the vermis, reducing the production of GABA – thus long-term stress makes a person much more on edge and exhausted

Endorphins and Enkephalins

- Brain opiates give sense of pleasure
- Their release is triggered by the dopamine system so when dopamine levels drop, it is much harder to feel joy
- These neurotransmitters are critical to social bonding

C.R.H. (corticotrophin-releasing hormone)

- Released by the amygdala to start the stress reaction
- Signals the locus coeruleus nucleus to release extra norepinephrine
- Signals via the hypothalamus and the pituitary gland for the adrenal glands on the kidneys to release cortisol, epinephrine (also called adrenalin) and norepinephrine (also called noradrenalin)

Glutamate

- The brain's primary neurotransmitter
- Involved in psychosis, anxiety, stress, addiction and pain
- New drugs are still being designed to modulate glutamate action

NEUROTRANSMITTERS

There are FIVE classes of neurotransmitters:

1.   **Acetylcholine**

2.   **Biogenic Amines**

(a)   catecholamines   - dopamine
                           - norepinephrine
                           - epinephrine

(b)   indolamines   - serotonin
                           - histamine

3.   **Amino Acids**
     -   GABA (gamma-aminobutyric acid)
     -   Glycine
     -   Aspartate
     -   Glutamate

4.   **Peptides (strings of amino acids)**
     -   Endorphins
     -   Enkephalins
     -   Others including CRH (corticotrophin-releasing hormone)

5.   **Other**
     -   ATP
     -   Nitric oxide
     -   Carbon monoxide

New neurotransmitters are still being discovered

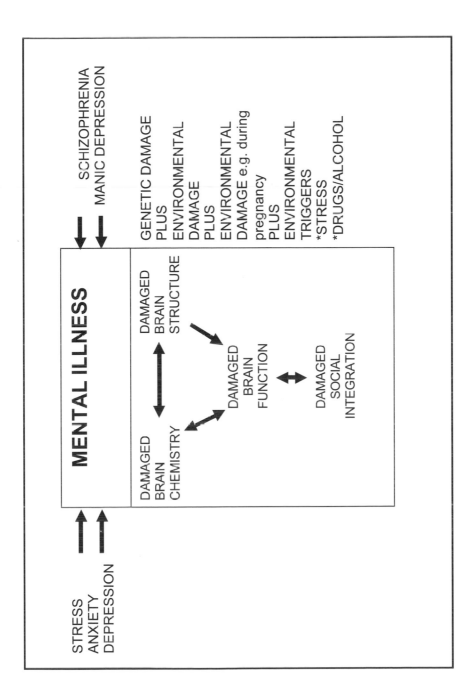

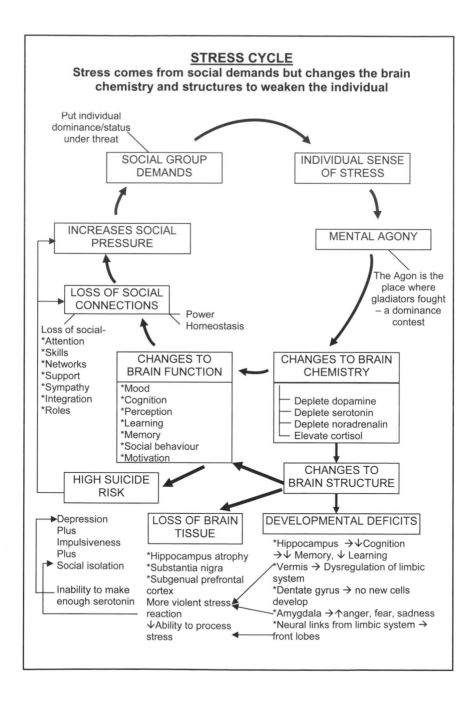

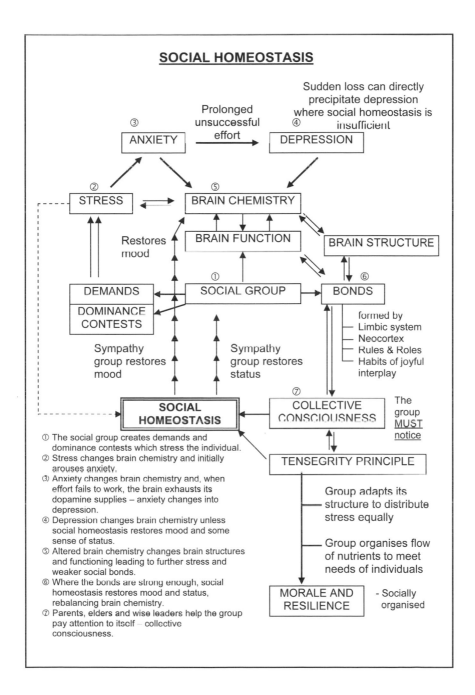

SOCIAL HOMEOSTASIS

① The social group creates demands and dominance contests which stress the individual.
② Stress changes brain chemistry and initially arouses anxiety.
③ Anxiety changes brain chemistry and, when effort fails to work, the brain exhausts its dopamine supplies – anxiety changes into depression.
④ Depression changes brain chemistry unless social homeostasis restores mood and some sense of status.
⑤ Altered brain chemistry changes brain structures and functioning leading to further stress and weaker social bonds.
⑥ Where the bonds are strong enough, social homeostasis restores mood and status, rebalancing brain chemistry.
⑦ Parents, elders and wise leaders help the group pay attention to itself – collective consciousness.

THREE MAIN FACTORS IN ANXIETY AND DEPRESSION

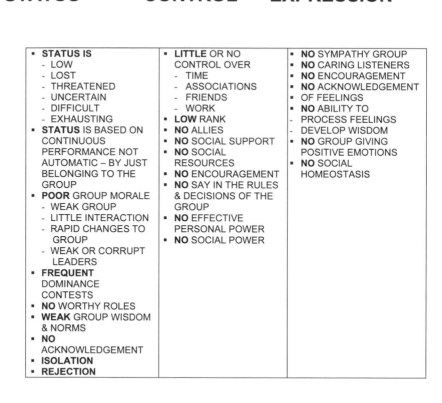

ANXIETY ➤ DEPRESSION

- HOPEFUL
- AROUSED
- HIGH
  - DOPAMINE
  - NOREPINEPHRINE
- NORMAL SEROTONIN

STRESS

- HOPELESS
- EXHAUSTED
- DEPLETED
  - DOPAMINE
  - NOREPINEPHRINE
  - SEROTONIN

WEAK STATUS   WEAK CONTROL   WEAK EXPRESSION

- **STATUS IS**
  - LOW
  - LOST
  - THREATENED
  - UNCERTAIN
  - DIFFICULT
  - EXHAUSTING
- **STATUS** IS BASED ON CONTINUOUS PERFORMANCE NOT AUTOMATIC – BY JUST BELONGING TO THE GROUP
- **POOR** GROUP MORALE
  - WEAK GROUP
  - LITTLE INTERACTION
  - RAPID CHANGES TO GROUP
  - WEAK OR CORRUPT LEADERS
- **FREQUENT** DOMINANCE CONTESTS
- **NO** WORTHY ROLES
- **WEAK** GROUP WISDOM & NORMS
- **NO** ACKNOWLEDGEMENT
- **ISOLATION**
- **REJECTION**
	- **LITTLE** OR NO CONTROL OVER
	  - TIME
	  - ASSOCIATIONS
	  - FRIENDS
	  - WORK
	- **LOW** RANK
	- **NO** ALLIES
	- **NO** SOCIAL SUPPORT
	- **NO** SOCIAL RESOURCES
	- **NO** ENCOURAGEMENT
	- **NO** SAY IN THE RULES & DECISIONS OF THE GROUP
	- **NO** EFFECTIVE PERSONAL POWER
	- **NO** SOCIAL POWER
		- **NO** SYMPATHY GROUP
		- **NO** CARING LISTENERS
		- **NO** ENCOURAGEMENT
		- **NO** ACKNOWLEDGEMENT
		- OF FEELINGS
		- **NO** ABILITY TO
		- PROCESS FEELINGS
		- DEVELOP WISDOM
		- **NO** GROUP GIVING POSITIVE EMOTIONS
		- **NO** SOCIAL HOMEOSTASIS

HOW OUR VULNERABILITY VARIES (1)

In every social group, individuals vary in their level of dependency and vulnerability. They vary in two distinct ways.

First, individuals vary in their intrinsic dependency and vulnerability.

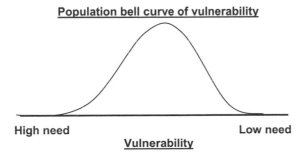

Population bell curve of vulnerability

High need   **Low need**

Vulnerability

Second, within each individual's life, life events, including loss, crises and periods of stress or rapid change, increase their dependency and vulnerability for a period of time.

Variations in lifetime vulnerability - example

As the level of individual dependency and vulnerability increases, their well-being needs increase. The degree of social integration which the group achieves and maintains as the current norm, and the level of production of nutrients and morale, determines the group's capability to meet the spectrum of individual vulnerability and need.

HOW OUR VULNERABILITY VARIES (2)

When we are here
we have high needs for
social homeostasis
-sympathy
-support
-power

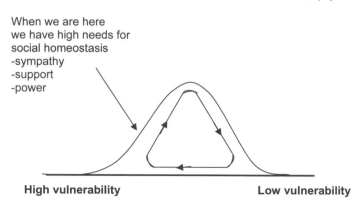

High vulnerability   **Low vulnerability**

We move inside the bell curve at different times

25% Australian teenagers

17.1% London UK

2.9% Spain

0% Tribal village
PNG

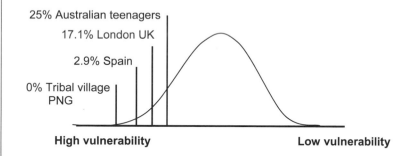

High vulnerability   **Low vulnerability**

As social stress exceeds social homeostasis
more people develop clinical depression

SOME FACTORS WHICH INCREASE STRESS

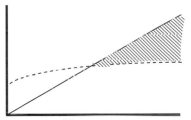

Personal expectations of success, ownership, status, etc.

Competence

Time

1. Personal performance expectations exceed competence

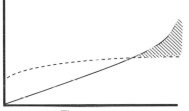

Difficulty of performance demanded by social group

Competence

Time

2. Group performance demands exceed competence

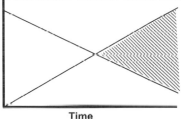

Difficulty of performance demanded by social group

Security of status in social group

Time

3. Performance demands increase as security decreases

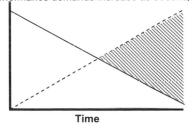

Combined personal and social demands

Social homeostasis: power of the group to restore sense of happiness, worth and well-being

Time

4. Performance demands increase as social homeostasis decreases

SOCIAL INTEGRATION, MORAL REGULATION, WELL-BEING AND SUICIDE

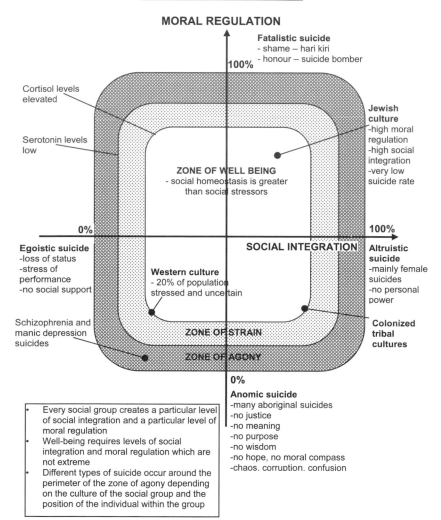

MORAL REGULATION

Fatalistic suicide
- shame – hari kiri
- honour – suicide bomber

100%

Cortisol levels elevated

Serotonin levels low

Jewish culture
-high moral regulation
-high social integration
-very low suicide rate

ZONE OF WELL BEING
- social homeostasis is greater than social stressors

0%

SOCIAL INTEGRATION

100%

Egoistic suicide
-loss of status
-stress of performance
-no social support

Altruistic suicide
-mainly female suicides
-no personal power

Western culture
- 20% of population stressed and uncertain

Colonized tribal cultures

Schizophrenia and manic depression suicides

ZONE OF STRAIN

ZONE OF AGONY

0%

Anomic suicide
-many aboriginal suicides
-no justice
-no meaning
-no purpose
-no wisdom
-no hope, no moral compass
-chaos. corruption. confusion

- Every social group creates a particular level of social integration and a particular level of moral regulation
- Well-being requires levels of social integration and moral regulation which are not extreme
- Different types of suicide occur around the perimeter of the zone of agony depending on the culture of the social group and the position of the individual within the group

TEN TIPS FOR TEACHERS TO
BUILD STUDENT WELL-BEING

1.   Use well-being strategies to help parents with parenting.

2.   Use the framework of strategies and knowledge to directly build students' well-being - not just wait.

3.   Help students build social capital and social networks to make their sense of status more secure and broadly based.

4.   Help students raise their social homeostasis and consciously raise their nutrient flows of joy, love, wisdom and empowerment.

5.   Build positive interdependence using co-operative learning teams, etc.

6.   Help students share their wisdom and plan to make life better for themselves and each other.

7.   Help students build their morale by coming up with good ideas and contributing to the well-being of themselves, the whole class, the school, their families, their communities, the environment, the earth, etc.

8.   Students can:
      - share friendship skills
      - plan and carry out good ideas, e.g. co-operative teams could compete on weight loss
      Schools can:
      - help students experience synergy and idealism
      - create better neighbourhood

9.   Do some regular team teaching:
      - with another teacher
      - with a student (older)
      - with a student from the class
      -

10.   Invite a different meditation or yoga teacher to give a class or talk once a term to help students learn to turn their minds inward as well as outward.

TEN STRATEGIES FOR SCHOOLS TO DIRECTLY FOSTER WELL-BEING

1. Build the creation and maintenance of well-being into the school curriculum and activities.

2. Act as the dominant institution of culture in the community and build community connectedness and social capital, and facilitate continuous co-creativity involving children of all ages and adults from all sectors of the community.

3. Recognise that children are making their lives now, not just studying for future lives, and directly help them build their lives and their social fabric of kith and kin and community.

4. Structure school educational activities to build positive interdependence and mutual skill-sharing, particularly across age divisions, by co-operative learning, coaching, etc.

5. Adapt school size and group structures to fit human biological design, e.g. 150 student schools or sections, better and more stable groups in high school ,etc.

6. Help students plan and co-create their own well-being and use eldership energies – to get older students to help younger students.   Use friendship circles and nurture groups, class discussions, etc.

7. Revitalise sports and PE by putting more fun into it, for example, get class-class competitions around fitness – get local government/ businesses to donate good prizes, etc. Base PE on play.

8. Teach parents about ways to strengthen well-being.

9. Help students 'recapture' their communities. Use the collective power of students as the biggest daily gathering in their community to come up with ways to build positive community.

10. Teach students about well-being, about nutrients and morale, teach friendship and other social skills and foster a more conscious culture of mutual encouragement, care and empowerment.

<u>CREATING POSITIVE INTERDEPENDENCE</u>

Ten types:

1. GOAL → Common purpose established. One achieves if all achieve.

2. REWARD → All team mates receive the same reward if every team mate succeeds.

3. RESOURCE → One set of materials per group.

4. ROLE → Each member is assigned a complementary and interconnected role.

5. SEQUENCE → Overall task divided into sub-units and performed in set order.

6. SIMULATION → Team mates work through a hypothetical situation to succeed and/or survive.

7. CO-CREATION → Group co-operates to create and develop an idea, project or activity.

8. OUTSIDE FORCE → Groups compete against an outside force.

9. ENVIRONMENTAL → Group members are bound together by the physical environment.

10. IDENTITY → Team mates establish a mutual identity through group name, flag, motto, song, etc.

Adapted from Rolmeiser Bennett, B. Bennett & L. Stevahn

Glossary

Agon - (from Ancient Greek) the place where gladiators fought to the death or to defeat, so any place where an individual feels in a dominance contest, where their performance will change their status.

Agony/mental agony - the extreme negative mixture of emotions and thoughts when a person feels defeated by a situation and powerless to respond. Mental agony drives people to self-medication with drugs or alcohol, to murder, self-harm or suicide.

Aggression - (1) all actions to achieve dominance. (2) behaviours and attitudes that reflect rage, hostility and willingness to do verbal or physical damage - usually as a response to a perceived threat.

Amygdala - two almond-shaped clusters of nuclei in the limbic system which orchestrate the fight or flight response and store unconscious emotional memories.

Anomic suicide - suicide due to a lack of meaning, wisdom, moral structure and clarity in the social group.

Anomie - an absence of norms in a social group or culture, due to chaos, corruption, colonization or social upheaval, often caused by rapid economic change.

Anxiety - an emotional state of arousal caused by uncertainty - usually about status and control. High levels of dopamine and norepinephrine are released in the brain and can become depleted, leading to stress and depression.

Automatic status - status which a social group can give automatically - particularly to children, just for belonging to the group. Very important for children's security and wellbeing.

Biological design envelope - the concept that humans evolved to fit into certain size and patterns of social organization, and when people are put into social situations well outside these evolutionary 'designs', they suffer stress and other forms of ill health.

Cerebellum - part of the brain at the back, below the occipital lobes, responsible for fine motor coordination. It includes the vermis - a major source of GABA, which calms the limbic system.

Chaos - a self-perpetuating state of social disorganization which occurs when the moral regulation of a social group fails. Often expressed in violence, sexual and domestic abuse, feuds, drug and alcohol abuse, and corruption.

Co-creativity - the essential feature of healthy social play and healthy social groups. Children and/or adults cooperating to create mutual pleasure and benefit together.

Cortisol - the stress hormone, produced in the adrenal cortex on top of each kidney, and triggered by the fight or flight response to a perceived threat by the amygdala and other limbic system nuclei. It changes the body's metabolism, and damages both brain and body, if stress is chronic.

Culture - the oldest human science - the knowledge and behaviours by which a social group maintains its well-being and adapts to its environment and circumstances.

Demoralisation - a loss of confidence in the purpose, value, wisdom, competence or fairness of a group and its leaders. Western culture as it grows more competitive, individualistic, consumerist and ecologically destructive, is demoralizing to many young people, including children.

Deepest common denominators - just as in mathematics, fractions can be added by finding the lowest common denominators, divided communities and human groups can be brought together by finding the deepest common denominators, such as a shared concern for the well-being of their children, a common fear of youth suicide, or a shared dislike of street crime.

Depletion - the three neurotransmitters which generate arousal, motivation and mood, norepinephrine, dopamine and serotonin, are each secreted in nuclei about the size of a pea. Sustained anxiety, stress or depression rapidly depletes these nuclei. Clinical depression involves neurotransmitter depletion.

Depression - low spirits

> **Clinical depression** - depressed mood or loss of interest or pleasure in nearly all activities for two weeks or more; plus four of seven additional symptoms must be present: disruption in sleep, appetite or weight, energy, concentration, agitation or flatness, excessive guilt or feelings of worthlessness, thoughts of suicide. Clinical depression may be mild, moderate or severe. Suicide risk increases with severity and duration.

Depression rate - or incidence of depression: the percentage of the population of a group or area who are clinically depressed at any one time, usually within a twelve-month period. This rate varies widely between different cultures, but is stable within a group until there is social change.

Dominance - superior power. Humans naturally organize themselves within their social group into competitive dominance hierarchies.

Dominance contest - a fundamental human behaviour and preoccupation. A competition or ritual combat where someone wins, and someone is defeated. Brain chemistry changes neurotransmitter levels massively in each contestant before, during and after the fight or contest.

Dopamine - neurotransmitter involved in desire, motivation, anxiety and pleasure seeking. Dopamine levels are altered by most drugs of addiction. Psychosis, schizophrenia and manic depression involve abnormal dopamine levels.

Elders the group of adults in any social group who collectively take responsibility for maintaining the well-being of the group, watching how the group members and their relationships are, organizing the cultural activities, transmitting wisdom and containing unwise behaviour.

Empowerment - actions which build up a child's sense of their own inner power, as well as help them develop socially organized power to achieve their goals and protect them from social pressures and stress.

Endorphins - sometimes called beta-endorphins - peptide neuro-transmitters that have opiate-like behaviour, give pleasure and block pain; part of the brain's reward system.

Enkephalins - a related class of peptide neurotransmitter with opiatelike behaviour, giving pleasure and blocking pain; part of the brain's reward system.

Epinephrine - catecholamine neurotransmitter, also called adrenaline, produced by the adrenal glands on top of the kidneys; involved in the fight or flight response, raising the heartbeat.

G.A.B.A. - gamma-amino butyric acid, the primary neuroinhibitor in the brain, mainly produced in the vermis, it calms the limbic system. Some tranquillizers work by increasing G.A.B.A.

Globus pallidum - 'pale globe', two nuclei, one on each side of the thalamus next to the putamen nuclei, the globus pallidum produces endorphins and enkephalins, distributed through the frontal and prefrontal lobes and the cingulate gyrus.

Hippocampus - two symmetrical organs in the limbic system which created and store new conscious emotional memories. Each hippocampus has many cortisol receptors and chronic stress, including depression, causes significant loss of neurons, leading to difficulties in learning, thinking and memory.

Homeostasis - dynamic mechanisms by which the body maintains a constant internal environment.

Individual homeostasis - the internal mental behaviours, the biochemical adaptation and the individual actions by which a person on their own seeks to adapt to stress and maintain emotional well-being.

Social homeostasis - all the socially organized strategies and actions by which social groups and individuals in a social group share power and sympathy to adapt to stress and maintain emotional well-being.

Inner vastness - the experienced profound nature of the self, not as personality or history or set of habits or character, but as a living emptiness, in which all experiences and emotional states appear and disappear. Also called ocean of consciousness. Children often realize their profound nature between the ages of 9 and 13, and see adults in denial of this as 'muggles'.

Limbic system - an interconnected set of organs and clusters of nuclei at the top of the brain stem, underneath the cortex, the limbic system organizes the defence, arousal and aggression of the individual, by monitoring perception and cognition, and altering the neurotransmitter delivery system.

Locus coeruleus - the nucleus in the brain stem which produces norepinephrine, increasing mental focus and arousal.

Magic - a natural part of the spectrum of human logic concerned with moving powers and qualities between like objects to alter or defend social dominance. Consumer capitalism is largely fuelled by magic transactions, transfers and transformations.

Manic depression - also called bipolar disorder - a serious mental illness involving genetic developmental brain damage, which can vary greatly in severity and impact. It can be triggered by stress or psychoactive drug use. The individual experiences mood swings, and can experience psychosis, mental confusion and mixed episodes of irritability and depression at the same time. About 0.9% of every population has manic depression.

Moral regulation - one of the two primary requirements for any social group, the other being social integration. The set of norms and rules by which individuals are organized, judged and ruled, usually drawn from a divine authority or a set of moral precepts. They set out the guidelines for dominance and submission, cooperation and competition.

Morale - the amalgam of commitment, common purpose, confidence and cooperative competence which brings people together in a team or family or social group, determined and able to put their very best into a task, regardless of the danger, pain or difficulty.

Neurotransmitter - any of over 100 different chemicals which assist in sending a chemical or electrical signal from one neurone to another.

Norepinephrine - also called noradrenaline - a powerful neurotransmitter produced by the locus coeruleus which increases mental arousal and focus as part of the response to stress; high levels present are in anxiety until depletion leads to depression.

Primary prevention - strategies for preventing people becoming clinically depressed.

Secondary prevention - strategies for diagnosing and treating clinical depression.

Tertiary prevention - strategies for detecting and treating people in crisis, such as a breakdown, suicidal ideation, psychosis.

Putamen - two oval nuclei in the limbic system which, lying against each globus pallidum, on either side of the thalamus, look like a pair of lenses, so they are also called the lentiform nuclei.

Raphe nucleus - two nuclei which produce serotonin. The dorsal raphe nucleus, near the top of the brain stem, supplies the limbic system and cortex, while the raphe magnus nucleus, below it, supplies the cerebellum.

Schizophrenia - the most feared mental illness, it occurs in all human groups at about 1% of the population. Like manic depression, it is a genetic developmental disease, usually diagnosed as the brain reaches full development. It involves loss of brain tissue, but varies widely in severity, age of onset, response to treatment and frequency of psychotic episodes.

Self - the self is not the mind; you are not your thoughts and memories and waves of emotion. Many religious traditions teach self-realisation. Western economic and educational cultures, because they are powered by emotional states and emotional attachments, avoid self-realisation. But the kingdom, as Jesus said, is within.

Serotonin - the main neurotransmitter affecting mood. It is inextricably linked to social integration and status. Loss or status or isolation causes serotonin levels to drop. Brains of people who have committed suicide reveal structural changes in the prefrontal cortex and the raphe nucleus seeking extra serotonin.

Social maps - the brain makes maps of the social groups which the individual is a part of and continuously upgrades these social maps to keep track of the dominance rankings and alliances and to enable them to construct hypothetical calculations to gauge the effects of possible actions, including consumer purchases, clothes choices, and other dominance displays.

Sociobiochemistry - a new concept - that the social structures and relationships which ensure our well-being are formed and held together by the shared patterns of brain chemistry - when we share joy and affection our brains change to store and be sensitive to these memories of arousal and pleasure, eliciting endorphins, enkephalins, oxytocin, serotonin, dopamine and norepinephrine, and linking us to the people who were a part of this joy.

Sociobiology - a field of science synthesized by E.O. Wilson in 1976, linking sociology and biology, chemistry, evolution and eventually the humanities.

Spirits - an old term, very easy to use with children - you can see how their spirits are, high or low, and act to keep them high.

Status - place and rank in a social group.

Automatic status - place, rank and worth given by some social groups automatically to every member.

Performance status - status dependent on performance, usually in some form of dominance contest. It requires relative competence and the opportunity to perform - children and unemployed or displaced people are often excluded.

Stress - pressure that puts strain on the biological system. For humans, stress almost always involves a threat to status or control.

Substantia nigra - literally the 'black substance' - dark nucleus in the brain stem which produces dopamine.

Suicide - fatal voluntary self-harm, to relieve mental agony or distress, to end shame, or to increase the honour of the group, or to relieve the group of a burden.

Altruistic suicide – suicide due to excessive social integration, the individual is nothing.

Anomic suicide - suicide due to loss of meaning, purpose and hope.

Egoistic suicide - suicide due to excessive social isolation, loss of status, reputation, connection, chronic stress due to performance demands beyond one's competence, no social homeostasis.

Fatalistic suicide - suicide due to total predominance of moral order and regulation; shame suicides - hari kiri; honour suicides - suicide bombers.

Symbolic omnivore - humans consume things primarily for their meanings not for their nutritional value. The problem is that symbolic appetite is not finite, nor can it be sated.

Sympathy group - normally the 8-15 people who care strongly about each other, give each other sympathy and share their power and resources. The main source of social homeostasis.

Synergy - the cooperative energy which comes out of a group working together with shared enthusiasm - very important for children to experience early and in adolescence.

Tensegrity - a key property of flexibly linked members, like a group of friends, where a stress on any one point causes the whole structure to change shape, to share the stress equally among the members.

Thalamus - a large nucleus containing several smaller nuclei at the centre of the limbic system. It acts like a relay for sensory inputs to the brain, distributing signals to the cortex.

Transmission of wisdom - the many ways human groups and cultures distribute their wisdom to the members and down to the next generation.

Ventromedial frontal lobe - low area of prefrontal cortex responsible for the social emotions including shame, embarrassment and compassion.

Vermis - worm-like central structure linking the two hemispheres of the cerebellum; produces G.A.B.A.

Well-being model - model of well-being used in primary prevention where nutrients and morale are created and distributed by facilitating effective social integration and moral regulation.

Wisdom - the skills, knowledge and social structures by which wellbeing is maintained.

Yorro-yorro - the organizing principle of the actions of elders - it means everything standing up alive in spirit - every individual, every species, every population, every ecosystem: a timeless concept already 40,000 years old.

Bibliography

Anatomy of Melancholy, C. Gorman, p.59, *Time*, 5/5/97.

Animals at Play (article), *National Geographic*, 9/94.

Antidepressants have little more effect than placebos, J. Bowbotham, p.7, *Sydney Morning Herald*, 21/10/02.

Bowling Alone, The Collapse and Revival of American Community, R. Putnam, Simon and Schuster, N.Y. 2000.

Brain, repair yourself – how the brain makes new neurons, F. Gage, pp.28-35, *Scientific American*, 9/03.

Concentrate the healers, J. Buckell, p.33, *The Australian*, 12/6/02.

Consilience, The Unity of Knowledge, E.O. Wilson, Knopf, N.Y. 1998.

Concise Colour Medical Dictionary, ed Martin, 3rd ed, O.U.P. Oxford, 2002.

Dealing with Death and Suicide in the School Community, Department of Education, Queensland, Aust, 1992.

Decoding schizophrenia, D.C. Javitt J.T. Coyle, pp.38-45, *Scientific American*, 1/04.

Depression and the birth and death of brain cells, Jacobs, Praag and Gage, pp.340-345, *American Scientist*, Vol.88, 7/02.

Depression: Social and Economic Timebomb, ed Dawson and Tylee, W.H.O., BMJ, London, 2001.

Depressive disorders in Europe, Ayuso-Mateos et al, pp.308-316, *British Journal of Psychiatry*, 10/01.

Descartes Error, Emotion, Reason and the Human Brain, A.R. Damasio, Putnam, N.Y. 1994.

Diagnosing disorders, S. Hyman, pp.77-83, *Scientific American*, 9/03.

Diagnostic and Statistical Manual of Mental Disorders, 4th ed, American Psychiatric Press, Washington DC, 1994.

Divorce predictor is 94% accurate, T. Radford, p.8 *Guardian*, 13/2/04.

Emotional Intelligence, Why it can Matter More Than IQ, D. Goleman, Bloomsbury, London, 1996.

Friends: the secret to a longer life, K. Griffin, pp.132-137, *Readers Digest*, 9/02.

Gray's Anatomy, Gray, Senate, London, 1994.

How to take an antidepressant (article), *Psychology Today*, 1/03.

How we get addicted, A. Park, pp.52-58, *Time*, 5/5/97.

How your love life keeps you healthy, McCormick et al, pp.51-98, *Time*, 1/04.

Human Anatomy and Physiology, Carola et al, 2nd ed, McGraw-Hill, 1992.

In Search of Excellence, T. Peters and R. Waterman, Harpe and Rowe, London, 1982.

In the shadow of fear, P. Brown, pp.30-37, *New Scientist*, 6/9/03.

I think, but who am I? J. Grey, pp.46-49, *New Scientist*, 14/9/02.

Iron John: A Book About Men, Robert Bly, *Element*, 1991.

Kyogle Youth Action – Project X – Community: A Framework for Preventing Youth Suicide – Evaluation Theory, A.R. Willoughby, K.H.S. Aust, 1998.

Linking mind and brain in the study of mental illness, a project for a scientific psychopathology, N. Andersen, *Science Magazine*, May, 2003.

Mind Over Mood, Greenberger and Padesky, Guildford Press, N.Y. 1995.

Mystery of consciousness, J.M. Nash, pp.56-57, *Time*, 18/10/99.

Night Falls Fast: Understanding Suicide, K.R. Jameson, Vintage Books, 2000.

Psychiatric Nursing: Contemporary Practice, ed M. Boyd, Lippincott, Philadelphia, 2002.

Rethinking the lesser brain, Bower and Parsons, pp.40-47, *Scientific American*, 8/03.

S.A.L.T. Suicide Prevention Handbook, Robert Dunlop, Womens Day-Lifeforce, Australia, 2000.

Sick at heart, mental illness in Asia, pp.52-61, *Time*, 24/11/03.

Sociobiology, The New Synthesis, E.O. Wilson, Harvard UP, Cambridge, Mass, 1975.

Some kids are orchids, J. Garbarino, p.33, *Time*, 20/12/99.

Stress, J. Clark, Chandos, Oxford, 2002.

Suicide, A Study in Sociology, E. Durkheim, Routledge, London, 1996.

Suicide linked to pressure of HSC, J. Rowbotham, p.3, *Sydney Morning Herald*, 24/1/03.

Suicide Prevention, TAFE, Australia, 1995.

Suicide Prevention, Trainers Manual, S.P.A., Australia, 1996.

Taming stress, an emerging understanding of the brain's stress pathways points towards treatments for anxiety and depression beyond valium and prozac, R. Sapolsky, pp.67-75, *Scientific American*, 9/03.

Tell Me I'm Here, A. Dereson, Penguin, Melbourne, 1991.

The Affluent Society, J.K. Galbraith, Penguin, UK, 1979.

The architecture of life, D.E. Ingber, pp.30-39, *Scientific American*, 1/98.

The Blank Slate: The Modern Denial of Human Nature, S. Pinker, Allen Lane, 2003.

The Brain and Emotion, E. Rolls, O.U.P., UK, 2001.

The Different Drum, Community-making and Peace, M. Scott Peck, Rider, London, 1987.

The Feeling of What Happens, Body and Emotion in the Making of Consciousness, A.R. Damasio, Heinemann, London, 2000.

The 4 R's, Managing Youth Suicidal Behaviour: A Handbook for GP's, Australia, 1998.

The folly of a society that pensions off wisdom, Prof. M. Prior, *The Australian*, 16/3/94.

The neurobiology of depression, C.B. Nemeroff, pp.29-35, *Scientific American*, 6/98.

The new science of Alzheimers, J.M. Nash, pp.49-58, *Time*, 23/8/99.

The other half of the brain, R.D. Fields, pp.26-33, *Scientific American*, 4/04.

The Oxford Companion to the Mind, ed Gregory, O.U.P., Oxford, 1987.

The Path of Least Resistance, for Managers, Designing Organisations to Succeed, R. Fritz, McGraw-Hill, London, 1999.

The placebo effect, W.A. Brown, pp.68-73, *Scientific American*, 1/98.

The pleasure seekers, H. Phillips, pp.36-40, *New Scientist*, 11/10/03.

The Pursuit of Excellence, T. Peters, Audiobooks, 1986.

The pursuit of happiness, M. Bond, pp.40-47, *New Scientist*, 4/10/03.

The Road Less Travelled, A New Psychology of Love, Traditional Values and Spiritual Growth, Scott Peck, Hutchinson, London, 1983.

The secrets of autism, J.M. Nash, pp.50-60, *Time*, 6/5/02.

The Selfish Gene, R. Dawkins, O.U.P, 1989.

The Successful Self, Dorothy Rowe, Fontana, London, 1988.

The Tao of Leadership, John Heider.

The Tipping Point, How Little Things Can Make a Big Difference, Malcolm Gladwell, Little, Brown, London, 2000.

The value of positive emotions, B.L. Frederickson, pp.330-336, *American Scientist*, Vol.91, 7/03.

Virtue in mind, A.R. Damasio, p.48, *New Scientist*, 8/11/03.

Working With Mental Illness, D. Tilbury, Macmillan, London, 1994.

Why do some people get hooked on drugs and fatty foods? M. Szalavitz, p.23, *New Scientist*, 23/8/03.

Why? The neuroscience of suicide, C. Ezzell, pp.34-39, *Scientific American*, 2/03.

Index

Andrew Willoughby has worked as a researcher, teacher, community development facilitator and project coordinator since 1977. He has worked with children, youth and adults.

He was a co-founder of the Lismore Community School, the North Coast Adult Education Group and the Summerland Senior Adult Learning Centre. He has worked with Aboriginal communities to develop housing, youth services and training. In 1997-98 he co-ordinated an Australian government youth suicide prevention pilot project 'Project X', which won the New South Wales Premier's Award in 1998. This handbook is based on the prevention theory developed in the project.

Recently he has run workshops in UK on drug-free protection from depression, and has lectured and spoken on TV and radio. He works with families and communities to build well-being and prevent suicide.

He enjoys sailing and making (quite bad) music with his family and friends.